I BELIEVE

I BELIEVE

A Guide to
the Christian Faith
in the Apostles' Creed

ROBERT HALL

"Robert Hall spent most of his working life in the Bronx... and he knows people's blind spots. He knows how much pressure for social acceptance is drowning courage to find out and speak out *Christ's definition of a Christian*. What most people assume is Christian is *not* what Jesus and the Apostles taught, but simply some form of *moralistic therapeutic Deism* along these kinds of lines: God created the world; he wants us to be nice to one another, (taught somewhere in the Bible and by most world religions), and the central goal of life is to be happy, free from fear, and to feel good about oneself. God doesn't need to be particularly involved in one's daily life, unless there is an emergency. Good people go to heaven (whatever that might be) when they die. But if you're ready and honest enough, you'll do yourself a favor by absorbing *I Believe: A Guide to the Christian Faith in the Apostles' Creed* to get reminded of what the original followers of Jesus Christ knew was *the true Christian faith as taught by Christ and his Apostles*."
—Dr. Greg Livingstone, Founder, *Frontiers*, and EPC WO Senior Associate for Missions Advancement

"An absolutely great book for Sunday School class, new members' classes, etc. Bob has a real gift in explaining orthodox and complex ideas in layman's terms in an approachable way, while always backing things up with Scripture. He has obviously honed it in decades of front-line preaching to unregenerate and new believers, many of whom are not going to tackle theological tomes."
—Dr. David Ayers, Assistant Provost and professor of sociology, Grove City College

"Power needs parameters, or else it is misused or dissipated. The early church saw the power of the gospel framed by parameters in the Scriptures, and summarized those essential Christian truths in the Apostles' Creed. Robert Hall uses his skills as a seasoned scholar who has lived biblical truth for decades as a pastor at an inner-city church in New York City to write this book that examines and explains each part of the Apostles' Creed for the contemporary reader. This book displays the glories of the Father, Son, and Holy Spirit, and the basic Christian doctrines that define the church. This book will help each believer to focus on the foundational truths of the Christian faith that will empower one's daily walk with Christ."
—Jordan Lorence, Sr. Counsel, Director of Strategic Engagement, Alliance Defending Freedom

"Bob Hall has crafted a useful, faithful tool for shaping the solid rock of God's Word into an understandable sculpture reflecting the Rock of our salvation."
—JACK ROBERTS, Co-pastor of The Bronx Household of Faith (from the *Foreword*)

I Believe: A Guide to the Christian Faith in the Apostles' Creed
Copyright © 2020 by Robert G. Hall, Th.M

ISBN: 978-1-7343452-5-4

Unless otherwise noted, Scripture quotations are from the ESV®
(The English Standard Version®), copyright © 2001 by Crossway, a
publishing ministry of Good News Publishers. Used by permission.
All rights reserved.

Cover Design and typeset by www.greatwriting.org
Printed in the United States of America

Great Writing Publications
Taylors, SC
www.greatwriting.org

To my Jeannie

*My chiefest comfort
under heaven*

The Apostles' Creed

I believe in God, the Father Almighty,
maker of heaven and earth;
And in Jesus Christ his only Son, our Lord,
who was conceived by the Holy Spirit,
born of the Virgin Mary,
suffered under Pontius Pilate,
was crucified, died, and was buried;
he descended into hell;
the third day he rose again from the dead.
He ascended into heaven
and is seated at the right hand of God the Father Almighty.
From there he will come to judge the living and the dead.
I believe in the Holy Spirit,
the holy catholic church,
the communion of saints,
the forgiveness of sins,
the resurrection of the body,
and the life everlasting. Amen.

Table of Contents

Foreword 11

Introduction 13

I Believe in God 17

I Believe in God the Father 25

I Believe in God, the Father Almighty 29

I Believe in God . . . The Maker of Heaven and Earth 37

And in Jesus Christ His Only Son, our Lord 43

Who was Conceived by the Holy Spirit, Born of the Virgin Mary ... 59

Suffered Under Pontius Pilate 65

He Was Crucified, Died, And Was Buried 71

He Descended into Hell 77

The Third Day He Rose Again from the Dead 81

He Ascended into Heaven. 87

From There He Will Come. 93

I Believe in the Holy Spirit 97

I Believe in the Holy Catholic Church. 101

I Believe in the Forgiveness of Sins 109

I Believe in the Resurrection. 113

Conclusion 117

About the Author 119

Foreword

My close friend of fifty-four years has written a book that captures what he has devoted his life to: the gospel of Jesus Christ. Ever since we met at a missions' conference in 1966, Bob Hall has demonstrated a zealous passion to speak that good news into people's lives. Ministering and pastoring in the Bronx for forty-six years, he exhibited a commitment to speak the language of those whose social/economic/cultural background was unfamiliar to him because he longed for them to know his Savior. To cross those barriers, a messenger has to focus on the essentials of the message and seek to drive them home in the simplicity and directness of the Holy Spirit—simple, but not simplistic.

The genius of using the Apostles' Creed as a vehicle to illuminate the crucial components of the story of redemption, and illustrate how one embraces it personally, issues from a heart seasoned with decades of experience and energized by the compassion of a rescued soul. The eternal truths have to be translated into ordinary language and yet remain faithful to the God of revelation. Bob has done that in a way that is engaging and challenging, yet accessible to someone not familiar with Christian teaching.

The questions at the end of the manageable, easily-read chapters focus the point and provoke deeper thought on the profound truths presented. The suggested prayers concluding each section provide a pathway of response for the reader, encouraging him or her to do more than store information but to pursue a true, heart-knowledge of God. After all, the apostles' "creed" was an expression of authentic, life-altering faith in the crucified, resurrected and living Christ.

I Believe. . .

Bob Hall has crafted a useful, faithful tool for shaping the solid rock of God's Word into an understandable sculpture reflecting the Rock of our salvation.

Jack Roberts
Co-pastor of The Bronx Household of Faith, an urban church of the historic biblical persuasion and director of Hope Christian Center, for over fifty years, a residential discipleship ministry for men with life-controlling problems

1

Introduction

What do you believe? Is that too personal a question? None of my business, you say? You are certainly free to put this book down and read no further. I hope you won't, because this is the most important question you will ever face in life. I would go so far as to say that it is more important than finding the right school, choosing the right mate, or landing the perfect job.

I would like to think with you about what Christians believe. That might seem to you an impossible task. Your experience might be that different Christians believe different things: this Christian group and that Christian group seem to run around denouncing all the other groups as false. "Just follow us," they say, "because we're the *real* Christians; everybody else only has a part of the truth at best." How are you supposed to know? That's a very good question. I believe that it is one that can be answered.

Perhaps you have never concerned yourself about this. You're just trying to get through life, make a living, and have a good time without hurting anybody in the process. Most people are like you. You come home at the end of the day, grab some food off the stove, plunk yourself down on the couch, pull out your phone and scroll through social media updates, look at sports, or watch a movie. That's about it.

But deep down there are these nagging questions. You try not to think about them, but they pop up from time to time. It usually has something to do with guilt. What are you going to do with your guilt?—Oops! I'm getting ahead of myself; I said we were going to talk about what Christians believe, and you thought to yourself, "Which Christians? What is the true religion after all?"

Let me say that there is a way to answer this question once

I Believe. . .

and for all. Let us begin with another question: What is the authoritative source that will verify the claims being made here? The answer is quite simple. It is the Bible, God's holy Word. But since you are not at the place where you are able to go verse by verse through all sixty-six books of the Bible, we're going to have to take a different approach.

Nearly 2,000 years ago, when nobody had a personal copy of the Bible and not everyone could read, Christians put together a summary of Christian beliefs. This summary has been used down through the ages by Christians from different backgrounds. If you go through this summary, you will have a pretty good idea as to what it means to be a Christian—I mean a *real* Christian, as opposed to someone who might say something like, "Well, I'm not a heathen so I guess I must be a Christian," or "My parents are Christian, so I guess that makes me one, too."

I'm sure you'll agree that if someone claims to be a Christian, we expect that person to live like one.

Before proceeding, I would like to talk a little bit about some terminology that you may not be familiar with. We're going to begin each section with two words: *I believe*. This summary of Christian belief uses those words over and over. We will also be using the word *faith*. Actually, the words *faith* and *believe* are almost interchangeable. If a person believes, that person has faith. To have faith in someone or something is to believe in that person or thing. To believe, in the biblical sense of the word, is not merely to utter some religious words, or even to say something that might be true as far as the Bible is concerned. To believe, as the Bible uses the term, is to act on something. If I believed I could fly, I wouldn't just say it—I would start flapping my arms! Mind, there is a big difference between believing in a fantasy, like my being able to fly, and believing what God says in his Word, the Bible. To believe him is to act on what he says.

It is very important to keep this in mind as we go through this summary of what true Christians really believe. To believe something is to act on it.

Oh yes, and one more thing. I hope it doesn't keep you from reading this book, but if I am going to be honest with you, I have to tell you this at the outset: to believe these things is not a take-

Introduction

it-or-leave-it option. This is what God is *commanding* you to believe. It is a summary of what the Bible tells us is a true Christian.

Some things in this book may not be stated completely accurately. That's not on purpose. Any book written by people will say some things that might be taken wrongly. Maybe they weren't written with the appropriate emphasis or they don't quite fit in with the big picture.

That's why we have the Bible. It is our ultimate standard for truth. It is our sole authority. It is completely accurate because the people who wrote it were inspired by the Holy Spirit. It is without error. That's why every effort has been made to back up what is being said in these pages with quotes from Scripture. Scripture is our ultimate source of authority.

At the end of each chapter there will be an opportunity for further consideration to stimulate your thinking, and a prayer to motivate you toward further inquiry. The written prayers are meant to give some direction. They are not meant to be a substitute for your prayer, which, if it is genuine, must be from the conviction and the desires of your heart.

What follows is a tried and true, nearly 2,000-year-old summation of what we call the historic Christian faith. It is my prayer for you that, as you come to know the historic Christian faith, it will lead you to a personal faith in the Lord Jesus Christ.

Here is what most Christians throughout Christianity's 2,000-year history have believed:

> I believe in God, the Father Almighty,
> maker of heaven and earth;
> And in Jesus Christ his only Son, our Lord,
> who was conceived by the Holy Spirit,
> born of the Virgin Mary,
> suffered under Pontius Pilate,
> was crucified, died, and was buried;
> he descended into hell;
> the third day he rose again from the dead.
> He ascended into heaven
> and is seated at the right hand of God the Father Almighty.

I Believe. . .

> From there he will come to judge the living and the dead.
> I believe in the Holy Spirit,
> the holy catholic[1] church,
> the communion of saints,
> the forgiveness of sins,
> the resurrection of the body,
> and the life everlasting. Amen.

---

1 Catholic here means "universal."

2

I Believe in God

Most people believe in some sort of Supreme Being, some invisible reality that stands behind what we see around us. Yes, there are atheists, people who say there is no God, but they tend to be in a minority, and, if I may say it, they have a difficult time being consistent with their atheism. How does one say there is no God in a world made by him? It's difficult to say the earth is flat when one can travel far enough west and arrive at the same point from the east. To look at your smartphone is to assume that somebody made it. By the same token, looking at the world, it is difficult to believe that it just happened by chance. It has the attributes of being made by someone.

We are not talking, however, about a Being that is the product of human reasoning. To believe in God is much more specific and profound than the notion that this world needs a world maker. Remember, we go to our authoritative source, the Bible, to discover what a person is saying when he or she says, "I believe in God."

The first four words of the Bible state, "In the beginning God..." (Genesis 1:1). We will get back to what the rest of Genesis 1:1 says later, but first let us consider the meaning of these words. They are very important for what comes afterward.

This world—the entire universe for that matter—has a beginning. We describe it in words uttered in a frame of reference that we would call three-dimensional space and time. That is the reality in which we live and think. Since this world has a beginning (and no scientist today would dispute that), there is a point beyond which there was no space and time. There was—for want of a better word—nothing.

But wait! When there was nothing, there was God. He stands outside the boundaries of space and time. He is not constrained by them. He is eternal, without beginning and without end. "Before the mountains were brought forth, or ever you had formed the earth and the world, *from everlasting to everlasting you are God*" (Psalm 90:2, emphasis added).

Jesus met a woman at a well, a Samaritan woman with whom he spoke about the real meaning of life. In that discussion, he told her that God is spirit (John 4:24). How does one speak of a Being who is spirit? There are no words to describe God as he really is. It would be like putting him in a cage surrounded by "experts" who would scrutinize him—impossible! So here we have God who, in and of himself, is off the radar screen of our limited minds. We think in terms of space and time, but God is outside it. He is eternal. He is spirit. He doesn't have a body like we have.

Moses was a man who lived about 1,500 years before Christ. He met God in the wilderness by means of a bush that was on fire but not consumed. Moses asked him his name. In ancient times, to get the name of a deity was to be able to gain a measure of control over it. Having the god's name enabled one to call on it for help, something like getting a password to be able to hack into someone's bank account. God is not like that. He doesn't jump to our demands. Neither is he some cosmic tow truck in the sky, available only in emergencies. He is not someone to whom we only call when we're in trouble, as people frequently do, especially in times of crisis or when facing death. He simply said to Moses, "*I am who I am.*" He is the eternal, self-existent God. This is not to say that he is inaccessible—it's just that we need to get straight in our minds that God is God and each of us is but one of his creatures.

There's more about God. He tells us that there is no other god like him. He is unique. "I am the LORD; beside me there is no other" (Isaiah 45:18b). "I am the first and I am the last; besides me there is no god" (Isaiah 44:6b). That's quite a statement in this day and age, when it is assumed that you choose your religion the way one chooses cereal for breakfast—some like corn flakes, others prefer rice crispies. God says "No" to that way of thinking. To say "I believe in God" is to believe that he is the *only* God.

To drive this point home, God called a man, Abraham, to

leave his home in Mesopotamia (modern-day Iraq) to go and live in the land of Canaan (modern-day Palestine). God did this because at that time, with each succeeding generation, the knowledge of him was becoming more distorted and obscure. How would he address this problem? Each nation was concocting its own understanding of a god around whom they would organize and build their own traditions and culture. This kind of a god was merely a projection of themselves. In some cases those religious beliefs led to horrible practices, such as human sacrifice.

God promised Abraham that he was going to make a great nation from him. That nation became the nation of Israel. They were the special people of God. It was not that God found them more loveable than the other nations. Rather, he chose this nation to show the people around them that the God of Israel was the one true God. They would be the repository of the law of God and his promises. He did this so that the other nations would look at Israel and say that their God was the one true God. Since God cannot be seen, one way that people would be able to have an idea of the one true God would be for them to observe God's people living in obedience to him.

A little background is in order. The family of Abraham, through his sons Isaac and Jacob, became the nation of Israel. Jacob, whose other name was Israel, had moved his family to Egypt because of a famine in the land where they lived. They continued to live in Egypt long after Jacob had died. Over the next 400 years, this family grew to be a great nation inside Egypt. The Egyptian king, Pharaoh, fearing that these people would overpower him, made them slaves. God raised up Moses to lead them out of Egypt into the land of Canaan. This land was originally promised to their ancestor Abraham. This is the story called the Exodus. It is a beautiful picture of God's redemption—more on that later.

Moses told the people of Israel about God's purpose for them as they were about to enter the promised land and set up permanent homes:

> Keep them [God's commandments] and do them, for that
> will be your wisdom and your understanding in the sight

> of the peoples [the surrounding nations], who, when they hear all these statutes, will say, 'Surely this great nation is a wise and understanding people.' For what great nation is there that has a god so near to it as the LORD our God is to us, whenever we call upon him? And what great nation is there, that has statutes and rules so righteous as all this law that I set before you today?"
> *(Deuteronomy 4:6–8)*

God, who chose to reveal himself through the nation of Israel, did so to demonstrate that he is the one true God who rules over all the nations. In the Psalms he says, "Be still, and know that I am God. I will be exalted among the nations, I will be exalted in the earth!" (Psalm 46:10)

It is an insult to God to say that there are many gods, or that he is something other than what he has revealed himself to be in his Word, the Bible. He considers it betrayal, the same way a jealous wife would look upon her husband seeing another woman. He told his people Israel in ancient times, "You shall not go after other gods, the gods of the peoples who are around you—for the LORD your God in your midst is a jealous God—lest the anger of the LORD your God be kindled against you, and he destroy you from off the face of the earth" (Deuteronomy 6:14-15). These are strong words. They are not a matter of opinion, much less a matter of interpretation. Israel's God was the God over all of humanity whether people outside its borders recognized it or not. Israel was surrounded by many nations. Each nation had its own god. The God of Israel, the one true God, says that all these other gods are false. It makes him quite angry when he is represented as an animal or a star or a planet. You don't like it when people put words in your mouth that you didn't say or otherwise misrepresent you. God doesn't like it when people misrepresent him. In fact, he holds them guilty for doing so.

The Apostle Paul spoke to a group of Greek philosophers on Mars Hill in Athens, Greece. He told them, as he had observed all their carved images of many different gods, "We ought not to think that the divine being is like gold or silver or stone, an image formed by the art and imagination of man" (Acts 17:29). The

Athenian philosophers were wrong about their idea of God, as indicated by their statuary representation of their many gods. Any object that is formed by human hands, no matter if it is a statue, or, say, a bookcase, begins with an idea in the mind. We form an idea in our minds as to how we want this object to look, and then we proceed to make it. An image depicting a god is actually the maker's idea of god that he had in his mind. It was this idea that caused him to make the image. It is wrong to represent God as an animal or a human.

Even if we have never taken a statue or any other kind of image and made it an object of worship, we can still engage in the practice called idolatry. We can do this by forming our own ideas about God—and we can be sure that when they are *our* ideas, they are wrong. Why? The Apostle Paul says that it is our tendency to take what God reveals to us about himself and distort it or suppress it (see Romans 1:18). We all have this tendency to think of God the way we would like him to be, as opposed to the way he really is. We need to get our understanding about God from the words that God has spoken to us about himself in the Bible.

There is a single word that expresses what we have been saying, that there is no other god like him. The word is *holy*. *Holy* literally means separate, set apart, unique. Holy is what God is. What is that? His holiness! It sounds like a circular statement. Well—yes, it is. But how else do you explain someone who does not have a body like we have and is not a part of the space-time universe, such that there is nothing in this world that can be compared to him? You say he is...holy. Actually, God's holiness is much more. It also speaks of his purity; there is no defect, no evil in him whatsoever. It also assumes his authority over our lives. Even in these attributes, he stands alone; he is unique. Moses experienced something of the holiness of God when God appeared to him in a burning bush. The bush was on fire but it was not consumed, "And Moses hid his face for he was afraid to look at God" (Exodus 3:6b).

God's holiness also speaks of his loftiness and his supreme authority. The prophet Isaiah felt it even more strongly when he had a vision of God in heaven,

> In the year that King Uzziah died I saw the Lord sitting upon a throne, high and lifted up; and the train of his robe filled the temple. Above him stood the seraphim. Each had six wings: with two he covered his face, and with two he covered his feet, and with two he flew. And one called to another and said: "Holy, holy, holy is the LORD of hosts; the whole earth is full of his glory!" And the foundations of the thresholds shook at the voice of him who called, and the house was filled with smoke. And I said: "Woe is me! For I am lost; for I am a man of unclean lips, and I dwell in the midst of a people of unclean lips; for my eyes have seen the King, the LORD of hosts!"
> *(Isaiah 6:1–5)*

His experience of God's holiness was terrifying. When he had a glimpse of God in all his purity and holiness, it caused him to proclaim judgment on himself. That's the meaning of the phrase, "Woe is me." To see God in his absolute purity and supreme authority is like looking in a mirror with a bright light that exposes our own sinfulness. If there is but a tiny dark speck on a white linen table cloth, it will be seen immediately. The Apostle John's vision of the risen Christ was not unlike Isaiah's experience:

> Then I turned to see the voice that was speaking to me, and on turning I saw seven golden lampstands, and in the midst of the lampstands one like a son of man, clothed with a long robe and with a golden sash around his chest. The hairs of his head were white, like white wool, like snow. His eyes were like a flame of fire, his feet were like burnished bronze, refined in a furnace, and his voice was like the roar of many waters. In his right hand he held seven stars, from his mouth came a sharp two-edged sword, and his face was like the sun shining in full strength. *When I saw him, I fell at his feet as though dead.* But he laid his right hand on me, saying, "Fear not, I am the first and the last, and the living one. I died, and behold I am alive forevermore, and I have the keys of Death and Hades."
> *(Revelation 1:12–18, emphasis added)*

To say "I believe in God" and really mean it, then, is much more than the mere utterance of these four words. It is saying that God has his being from himself. He is self-existent. He doesn't depend on any life-giving source or any creature on the earth to complete himself. He is eternal. He is from everlasting to everlasting. He doesn't have a body like we have, and there is no one thing or person or being to which he can be compared. Any representation of God, such as in a picture or an image, would be wrong because there is no way that our limited minds can form a true image of one who is above and beyond us. He is who he is. He is holy. How, then, can we know this God? We will consider this later. Let us just say at this point that we are absolutely dependent on him to reveal himself to us.

Let's review what is being said thus far. If you would know the God of Scripture, if you would rightly confess, "I believe in God," this is what you are saying:

- *God is eternal.*

- *He exists in and of himself without depending on any external life-giving source.*

- *He has no limitations whatsoever.*

- *He is spirit and does not have a body like we have.*

- *He is totally unique, that is to say, he is holy; and his holiness is also about his supreme authority, perfection, and purity.*

- *Any information acquired about God must come from him.*

- *You are absolutely dependent on him to reveal himself to you.*

For Further Consideration

1. How can you be sure that your ideas of God are correct? Does it make any difference?

2. What does it say about us if we wait for tragedy to strike and then we call out to God? If we don't call out to him when things are going well, why bother praying to him in times of crisis?

Prayer

Almighty God, deep down in my heart I know that you are there. I confess that I have conjured up in my own mind what you are like, but I cannot be sure that my ideas of you are correct. I want to know you. Help me!

3

I Believe in God the Father

We want to carry forward what we have just learned about believing in God with the additional truth, "I believe in God, *the Father*." Some say that since God is the father of all, we are all, therefore, God's children. This is true in one sense only, and we have to be very careful what we mean.

God is the father of all in the sense that he is the progenitor of the human race. He created our first parents, and all of us are descended from Adam and Eve. "God formed the man of dust from the ground and breathed into his nostrils the breath of life, and the man became a living creature" (Genesis 2:7). There is a sacredness to human life inasmuch as God breathed into Adam the breath of life, something that he did not do with the animals. You are made in the image of God. As such, you are a thinking, feeling being, made to know God. That we have all come from one beginning, from God who created us, underscores not only the sacredness of human life but also his authority over every person on the face of the earth. "God looks down from heaven on the children of man to see if there are any who understand, who seek after God" (Psalm 53:2).

It is not as though God is merely looking through some cosmic porthole to see what's going on. His "looking down from heaven" is his command to everyone that they must acknowledge him as God. In another Psalm we read these words conveying the same thought: "Know that the LORD, he is God! It is he who made us, and we are his" (Psalm 100:3a). To know that the Lord, he is God, is not a matter of acquiring information in the way that someone learns facts such as that two plus two equals four. To *know*, in the biblical sense of that word, is to submit to God's authority over one's life. God is the father of his creatures in the sense that he is their creator.

There is another meaning to "I believe in God *the Father*." He is also the father of the redeemed. We will consider this in more detail later. It is important to make this distinction at this point: Not all God's children of creation are God's children by redemption. Only those who have received his Son, Jesus Christ, who was sent by the Father into the world to save sinners, have the right to call God their father. Consider the words of the apostle John: "He [Jesus Christ] came to his own, and his own people did not receive him. But to all who did receive him, who believed in his name, he gave the right to become children of God, who were born, not of blood nor of the will of the flesh nor of the will of man, but of God" (John 1:11–13). Since God has given *some* the right to be called children of God, it follows that not everyone is a child of God by redemption. He has one unique Son, who is eternally begotten of the Father. That Son is Jesus Christ. If you would be a son or daughter of God, you must be so by adoption. Therefore, not everyone has the right to call God "Father"! God gives that right to those who receive his Son whom he sent into the world.

Thus far, to say "I believe in God, the Father," is to say, "I believe in one eternal, self-existent being who is spirit, holy, pure, without any imperfection, and who stands in authority over all of creation, including my life, and thereby commands obedience from me." Also, to believe in God the Father is to acknowledge our need of redemption, because not all people are children of God by redemption; this work of redemption is connected to his only Son, Jesus Christ, who came into the world. We will consider this in greater detail when we come to the place where we speak directly about "Jesus Christ, his only Son our Lord." Let it be said in our discussion up to this point that not everyone has the right to address God as father, in the same way that I cannot call every older male that I meet "Father." I can only call someone Father if I am a son by birth or by adoption.

For Further Consideration

1. Given the fact that not everyone can address God as Father, where does this place you among his creatures made in his image?

2. To address God as Father is a sign of the issue of authority over your life. How do you respond to his authority?

Prayer

Almighty God, I'm feeling increasingly alienated in a world where groups of people are drawing the circle ever more tightly around their particular identity, claiming to possess knowledge inaccessible to everyone else. To know you as Father would liberate me from the shackles of exclusionism from the outside and turbulence within.

I Believe. . .

4

I Believe in God, the Father Almighty

We have already been implying that God is almighty. We add to that here. There are several ways to understand God as the Almighty. He is all powerful. There is no power in the spiritual realm or anywhere on earth that can stand against him or otherwise frustrate his purposes. This is true even for those who live their lives as if he didn't exist at all—out of sight, out of mind. In the final analysis, he will not be ignored; he will vindicate himself. At the end of the day, he will show himself indisputably to be in the right. He will do that for himself and for those who wholeheartedly follow him. He does that by means of a relationship with his people whom he has redeemed. This relationship is called a covenant and more will be said about this subsequently. At this point, let it be said that he is powerful enough to hold this relationship together.

Examples In The Bible

"Almighty" means just that: God is all mighty, or all powerful. You may have heard the story of Job in the Bible. He lived about 4,000 years ago, perhaps about the same time as Abraham. He was an upright man, but God allowed Satan to afflict Job in order to test him, to see if he would end up cursing God. It was a kind of contest between God and Satan. Job's story is the story of many who go through severe trials, like physical suffering, and who wonder why. God is referred to as the Almighty many times in this account. Job had come to believe that God is indeed Almighty—not in an academic or rote memory sense, but out of his own struggle with suffering—that God is indeed Almighty, even though he could not understand the reason. In the midst of his pain, he felt that God wasn't listening to him, because, if he *was* listening, God would understand that his suffering was unfair.

How did God answer Job? With an unusual challenge. He urged Job to try to find some cosmic perch, some place to stand outside of him, where he could look over God's shoulder, so to speak, in order to figure out what God does and why. This, of course, is impossible, but it had to be brought home to Job. And we must come to grips with this as well. Here are some of the questions God put to Job: "Who is this that darkens counsel by words without knowledge? Dress for action like a man; I will question you, and you make it known to me. Where were you when I laid the foundation of the earth? Tell me, if you have understanding. Who determined its measurements—surely you know! Or who stretched the line upon it?" (Job 38:2–5). God Almighty is powerful and this means that his will and ways are, more often than not, beyond our ability to comprehend.

After a lengthy reminder to Job of all that God has done in his creation and how it all works together like the moving parts of a fine watch, God simply says to Job, "Shall a faultfinder contend with the Almighty? He who argues with God, let him answer it" (Job 40:2). The apostle Paul, after a similar line of questioning God, says in a similar vein, "But who are you, O man, to answer back to God? Will what is molded say to its molder, 'Why have you made me like this?'" (Romans 9:20).

"God Almighty" means that he is all powerful and he does what he does, in many instances, for reasons known only to him. To say, "I believe in God Almighty" is to submit to his will and his ways for your life and in the world around you. As a child, I wanted malted milk balls, my favorite candy, every day. Instead, I was allowed to have them maybe two or three times a year, usually around holiday time. I couldn't understand why my parents wouldn't allow me to have them all the time. Their reasoning was quite reasonable. Malted milk balls were, at that time, too expensive, and to eat them every day would be bad for my teeth, not to mention my general health—but I could not fathom their reasons, only my desire. To believe in God means, in part, to turn our thinking inside out and to do things God's way because he says so. After all, he is God Almighty.

The fact that God is almighty means that, in the end, he will be proved right in his actions, even when we think that we know better than he. This means that he will be vindicated. Don't misunderstand—it is not as though God needs approval for what he does. The vindication is for us insofar as God's actions enable us to see his wisdom as to why he does things the way he does. Remember, we don't always know why God does what he does, but in some instances we do. In the book of Genesis, in chapters 37–47, we read the amazing account of Joseph, one of Jacob's twelve sons, a story that illustrates this principle quite well. Joseph's brothers are jealous of him because they think it unfair for him, as one who was not the firstborn, to receive a double portion of their father's inheritance. This normally went to the oldest son in those days. In response, Joseph's brothers engineer a plot whereby Joseph is sold into slavery in Egypt. The brothers then tell their father that Joseph has been killed by a wild animal. But through a series of circumstances, ultimately under the hand of God, Joseph ends up becoming the prime minister of Egypt, about twenty years after being sold into slavery. About that time, Joseph's brothers, the family of Jacob, facing starvation back in the land of Canaan, have no other recourse but to go to Egypt to purchase grain. They eventually recognize their brother Joseph and become afraid that he will take revenge on them. Joseph's response is stunningly on the mark: "So Joseph said to his brothers, 'Come near to me, please.' And they came near. And he said, 'I am your brother, Joseph, whom you sold into Egypt. And now do not be distressed or angry with yourselves because you sold me here, *for God sent me before you to preserve life*" (Genesis 45:4–5, emphasis added). In an equally remarkable statement, Joseph reassures his brothers, who wonder if he might yet kill them after their father, Jacob, passes away: "As for you, you meant evil against me, but God meant it for good, to bring it about that many people should be kept alive, as they are today" (Genesis 50:20).

The beautiful love story of Ruth is another example of God caring for someone who has become totally destitute. Elimelech and his wife Naomi, with their two sons, have moved to the neighboring land of Moab to escape the famine in Israel. There the sons have married Moabite women, one of whom is Ruth. Sadly, Naomi's husband and her two sons die. Naomi returns to her native Bethlehem with her widowed daughter-in-law, Ruth, who chooses to go with her. In a rather somber, if not despondent, tone, she informs the townspeople on her return that "the Almighty has dealt very bitterly with me" (Ruth 1:20b). But God was actually caring for her through Ruth, a Moabitess who had the courage to risk moving to a foreign land with her mother-in-law, albeit unaccompanied by a man—a vulnerable move in those days. The happy ending to the story is Ruth marrying Naomi's relative, Boaz, who restores Naomi's land and provides a son to continue the line into which the Messiah, Jesus, would eventually be born. "Then the women said to Naomi, 'Blessed be the LORD, who has not left you this day without a redeemer, and may his name be renowned in Israel!'" (Ruth 4:14). Here, Naomi properly understands that it was the hand of Almighty God that brought about the bitter circumstances of her life. What she could not see was her own vindication as well as God's. God had not abandoned her and she had not totally abandoned God. He provided for her, but, more than that, the son born to Ruth and Boaz was the grandfather of King David, whose greater son, that is, his descendent, would be none other than the King of kings, Jesus Christ. Something greater was happening in this story. Ruth, a pagan who came to believe in the one true God of Israel, is in the line of the Messiah, showing that the Messiah, Jesus Christ, came into the world for all people, not just the Jewish people.

The apostle Peter says the same thing about the crucifixion of Christ: "Him, [Jesus] being delivered by the determinate counsel and foreknowledge of God, ye have taken, and by wicked hands have crucified and slain" (Acts 2:23, KJV). Here is the ultimate vindication of God. Evil men, carrying out their plot, put Jesus to death, but their actions were ultimately in the hand of Almighty God to carry out his plan of redemption.

The fact that God is almighty tells us that there is no power that can stand against him. "There is no wisdom, no insight, no plan that can succeed against the LORD" (Proverbs 21:30, NIV).

He will be vindicated even through the wicked actions of people. God will be proven to have been right in the end. It is important to know this as we entrust our lives to him. If he is vindicated, so will those be who have put their trust in him.

Think of it. Even in the valley of tears that is this life, there is ultimate meaning and purpose because Almighty God is in control. You can really trust him. It is not that we wait for tragedy to strike and then we turn to God. Rather, to sincerely confess, "I believe in God Almighty," is to say in your heart, "Lord, I thank you I can trust you with my life no matter what happens."

Covenant

There is yet another important idea that connects with God Almighty. We have already mentioned the covenant. The covenant is the way God relates to all of his creation, and it is the way he relates to his people whom he has redeemed. The covenant *is* the relationship that God has with his people. There are many kinds of relationships, many levels of friendship, from mere acquaintance to close friends. A business partnership is a very defined relationship. A couple who are married have a precisely defined relationship. The bond between a man and a woman in marriage, at its very core, is a mystery. It is so special that ultimately it is difficult to describe in words. On the other hand, it is a relationship with a definite structure, with defined boundaries. These can be put into words. When someone says, "She is my wife" or, "He is my husband," that is a very tightly defined relationship. It is quite specific, and everyone understands that.

It is the same with God's covenant with his redeemed people. Ultimately there is mystery in the relationship, because there comes a point where one is at a loss for words to properly describe it. At the same time, this relationship, a covenant, is something you can talk about, because it has an identifiable structure. God comes to us and binds himself to us by means of a promise. We, in turn, must respond in obedience and faithfulness, knowing that, ultimately, God is the one holding the relationship together. This covenant consists of promise, obligations, and outward, visible signs. Marriage is a covenant. The couple exchange vows.

They make promises to each other. There are obligations that each must fulfill. There are also visible signs, such as a marriage license and a ring. Throughout the Bible, God uses the analogy of marriage to talk about his relationship with his people.

To say "I believe in God, the Father *Almighty*" (the Hebrew term is *El Shaddai*) is to enter into, or to be in, covenant with him. God is the initiator. He sets the terms of the relationship. He binds himself to us and we to him. There are visible signs of that covenant. Baptism is the initial sign, and the Lord's Supper, sometimes called Holy Communion, is the ongoing sign of that relationship. He is the initiator of the relationship, but it proceeds in a mutual fashion, while all the time he remains the guarantor of that relationship. The foundation of the relationship is the person and work of Jesus Christ, the eternal Son of God who came to earth to die for sinners.

In Genesis God appears to Abraham: "When Abram was ninety-nine years old the LORD appeared to Abram and said to him, 'I am God Almighty; walk before me, and be blameless, that I may make my covenant between me and you, and may multiply you greatly'" (Genesis 17:1–2). God had already initiated and confirmed the relationship with Abraham, as recorded in Genesis chapters 12 and 15. Now God approaches Abraham again with the obligations: "Walk before me and be blameless." Every relationship carries obligations. This is especially true of God's covenant relationship with his people. We should be quick to say at this point that Abraham had done nothing to earn God's favor. There was no merit reckoned to him that would obligate God to show favor toward him. God chose Abraham by his grace. Grace is God doing something for us that we do not deserve. He chose Abraham. He promised to bless him and he also promised him that all the families of the earth would be blessed through him. That blessing came nearly 2,000 years after Abraham, when his descendant, Jesus Christ, was born in Bethlehem.

The important point to remember here is that "God Almighty" refers to God as the one who is in covenant with his people. To say "I believe in God Almighty" is to say that I am in covenant with him and, motivated by his love, I feel obligated to fulfill the terms of the covenant while at the same time depending on him to hold the relationship together. He is both the initiator and the guarantor of the covenant, and within that covenant relationship, there are obligations to fulfill.

To believe in *God Almighty* is to be faithful to the one who is in covenant with us. Note how the following brings together "God," "the Father," and "Almighty"

> What agreement has the temple of God with idols? For we are the temple of the living God; as God said, "I will make my dwelling among them and walk among them, and I will be their God, and they shall be my people. Therefore go out from their midst, and be separate from them, says the Lord, and touch no unclean thing; then I will welcome you, and I will be a father to you, and you shall be sons and daughters to me, says the Lord Almighty."
> *(2 Corinthians 6:16–18)*

The words "I will be their God, and they shall be my people" are a concise description of what the covenant actually is. Sometimes it is shortened in Scripture by the use of the words "your God," or "the Lord your God," or "my people." It denotes a special relationship that happens because Jesus Christ died for the sins of his redeemed people and thereby sets his love upon them. To confess, "I believe in God, the Father Almighty," is to say that you belong to God, body and soul, in this relationship called a covenant. Since it is a covenant of love, you do not want to do anything that dishonors your Father. You want to live a life that shows that you belong to him. This is what it means to be separate, that is, to be holy.

As you can see, to say, "I believe in God, the Father Almighty" is more than mouthing words, as a schoolchild might do during the pledge of allegiance to a flag. It is a serious matter to say, "I believe in God, the Father Almighty." It means, or it ought to mean, that you are actively engaged in seeking God, in learning from him, and doing what he commands, because he is God Almighty and he controls the destiny of your life.

For Further Consideration

1. What kind of world would this be if God was not all mighty or all powerful such as in science, in human relationships, and the course of history? Suggest several realms, such as in science, in human relationships, and the course of history.

2. Since God is almighty, it follows that he holds the destiny of this world, your life and mine, in his hands. How does this affect the way we ought to live our lives?

Prayer

Almighty God, I confess that much of my life's activity is directed towards controlling everyone and everything around me. I know intellectually that that is impossible. I want to know in practice that all of my life is in your hands. Help me to believe that that is something good and furthermore it is the only way to live.

5

I Believe in God...
The Maker of Heaven and Earth

I Believe in God, the Father Almighty, Maker of Heaven and Earth

It should be apparent from what we have discussed about believing in God the Father Almighty that he is indeed the maker of heaven and earth. In Genesis 1:1 we read, "In the beginning, God created the heavens and the earth." The word "created" means that he created out of nothing. God spoke and it was so. He is, after all, Almighty God. With him nothing is impossible. For example, in the days of creation, he said things like, "'Let there be light,' and there was light" (Genesis 1:3) and, "'Let the waters under the heavens be gathered together into one place, and let the dry land appear.' And it was so" (Genesis 1:9). He continued to speak words of command, and whatever he commanded came into being until the entire world—indeed, the entire universe—was created. Remember, we said earlier that there was a time when there was nothing—but even when there was nothing, there was God. He is eternal. Creation, including humanity, has a definite beginning.

You may be asking, why did God do this? He did it for his own glory. His glory is anything that shows, displays, or sets before us his character, attributes, and power. It is the glory of a clock to tell the time. It is the glory of the sun to shine. As it is in the nature of a fountain to overflow its form, so it is in the nature of God to reveal his glory. "The heavens declare the glory of God, and the sky above proclaims his handiwork. Day to day pours out speech, and night to night reveals knowledge" (Psalm 19:1–2). Psalm 148 is dedicated to this very theme—all of creation is worshipping its Creator. Here is a representative sample:

> Praise the LORD from the earth, you great sea creatures and all deeps, fire and hail, snow and mist, stormy wind fulfilling his word! Mountains and all hills, fruit trees and all cedars! Beasts and all livestock, creeping things and flying birds!
> *(Psalm 148:7–10)*

Why should they all praise the Lord? "For he commanded and they were created" (Psalm 148:5b).

As this discussion has moved along, do you get the impression that this world is not about you? It's about God. To believe in God, maker of heaven and earth, means that we must locate the center of our lives someplace else besides ourselves. It must be in God himself. Self-absorption and self-centeredness is the source of most, if not all, problems in human relationships, for the simple reason that we are blind to it. We can see selfishness in others but not in ourselves. To believe in God, maker of heaven and earth, is a launching pad away from ourselves and our own agendas toward God and his concerns for this world.

To carry forward the theme of God being the center of creation, let us return to Mars Hill and the Apostle Paul's speech. He tells these philosophers,

> The God who made the world and everything in it, being Lord of heaven and earth, does not live in temples made by man, nor is he served by human hands, as though he needed anything, since he himself gives to all mankind life and breath and everything.
> *(Acts 17:24–25)*

Notice what is being said about God here. He is Lord of heaven and earth. He is its owner and supreme authority. We can merge these two concepts, ownership and authority, into one word—*sovereign*. In times past, this word was interchangeable with the title "king." We say God is sovereign over his creation. He is in absolute control of everything, including your life and mine. Paul goes on to say, "In him we live and move and have our being" (Acts 17:28a). There you have it. The very breath we take, the next beat of our hearts, is by God's permission. What's the point of all this? The Apostle urges his hearers to seek the Lord, to repent of their wrong ideas about God, because there is coming a day of resurrection from the dead and after that, judgment (see Acts 17:27, 30–31). When it comes right down to it, to say the words (and sincerely mean them), "I believe in God . . . maker of heaven and earth," is to declare a personal commitment to the God of the universe. It is something like an oath of allegiance insofar as one is recognizing that God is the rightful owner and ruler of everything because he made it.

> For every beast of the forest is mine, the cattle on a thousand hills. I know all the birds of the hills, and all that moves in the field is mine. If I were hungry, I would not tell you, for the world and its fullness are mine.
> *(Psalm 50:10–12)*

Moreover, it is acknowledging that he is all powerful because "he commanded and they were created" (Psalm 148:5). To speak the Andromeda galaxy into existence or to create a snowflake such that each one is unique is almighty power indeed! We can be sure that there is no one who is able to wrest this creation away from God. There is no one who can pop up from behind some cosmic boulder and take God by surprise. He is all powerful.

It is our natural disposition to want to be in control of our lives. We would like to get enough money to be comfortable and to be able to take nice vacations. If there is sickness along the way, there's certainly a pill or some medical procedure to fix it. When we get old, we want to be mobile, pain free, and of sound mind until that inevitable moment—well—we would like to die in our sleep without any pain or suffering. Religion? It's nice to have ceremony and rituals for births, weddings, and funerals. They have their place, kind of like a wall hanging, pretty, but not necessary to the structure of the house. You and I can identify with these attitudes. The problem is that they are far from the meaning of "I believe in God, the Father Almighty, maker of heaven and earth."

To say these words with sincerity and conviction requires that your thinking be turned inside out. You must ask God to enable you to see things from his point of view and then act on them. Stop acting like you are a god, able to pull the control levers of your life. Discard the false attitudes that have caused you to live in a manner that says, "I can do what I want, when I want, and I don't want anyone interfering with my life." Say to God that you now understand that he is God, you are but one of his creatures, and you absolutely depend on him for the very breath that you breathe. Say to God that you want to learn from him, because apart from his revelation of himself in the Scriptures, you now realize that you can know nothing about him. Examine the words of Psalm 139:1–10 to see if they are the conviction of your heart:

> O LORD, you have searched me and known me! You know when I sit down and when I rise up; you discern my thoughts from afar. You search out my path and my lying down and are acquainted with all my ways. Even before a word is on my tongue, behold, O LORD, you know it altogether. You hem me in, behind and before, and lay your hand upon me. Such knowledge is too wonderful for me; it is high; I cannot attain it. Where shall I go from your Spirit? Or where shall I flee from your presence? If I ascend to heaven, you are there! If I make my bed in Sheol, you are there! If I take the wings of the morning and dwell in the uttermost parts of the sea, even there your hand shall lead me, and your right hand shall hold me.

Here is a God from whom you can run but not hide. Here is a God who already knows everything about you. Therefore make it your business to know God. The Lord wants you to lay your life bare before him—and you need to know that he knows. There is nothing that can be hidden from him, least of all what is in our hearts and what we have done with our lives. Here are more words from the prophet Isaiah along the same theme:

> I am the LORD, and there is no other, besides me there is no God; I equip you, though you do not know me, that people may know, from the rising of the sun and from the west, that there is none besides me; I am the LORD, and there is no other. I form light and create darkness; I make well-being and create calamity; I am the LORD, who does all these things.
> *(Isaiah 45:5–7)*

Notice here what the Lord is saying: "Every other god is a fake, a pretender. There is only one true God." None of the events of this world, down to the very details of your life and mine, is outside of his sovereign control.

If you would sincerely confess from your heart, "I believe in God, the Father Almighty, maker of heaven and earth," here is what you are saying: There is only one God, who made the universe, who also holds it together but stands outside it insofar as he is not caught up in the machinery of natural laws which he made as part of his creation. He is spirit and does not have a body like we have. What we know of God must come from him and his revelation of himself in the Scriptures. As maker of heaven and earth, he is its owner and authority; these are ideas combined in the word "sovereign."

God is commanding you to give up your autonomy (being a law unto yourself) and bow before him since he is Creator and you are the creature. There is more to know, but without this proper Creator-creature alignment, nothing that follows will make any sense. Bear in mind that "'God opposes the proud but gives grace to the humble.' Humble yourselves, therefore, under the mighty hand of God" (1 Peter 5:5b–6a).

For Further Consideration

1. What would be the effect if there was even a tiny patch of this universe outside the sovereign control of God?

2. One time a man from another religion said to me, "Oh, you only have one God." What does it say about any one particular god in his religion, if there are many gods, even millions of them? What kind of a world would this be?

3. What are the implications for you of God's exclusive claim of ownership over this world and its affairs, as well as over your own life?

Prayer

Almighty God, I confess that I have been living my life my way, viewing the world around me as a collection of things to grab for my gratification, oblivious to the fact that this is your world because you made it and hold everything together. I repent of this self-centered attitude and I come to you, acknowledging your rightful authority over my life. Given the fact that I can know nothing of you apart from what you have revealed about yourself in the Scriptures, I now take my rightful place as one made in your image, a creature of Almighty God, bowing before, and submitting to, your rightful ownership over my life. Furthermore, I confess that you are the only God, and beside you there is no other.

6

AND IN JESUS CHRIST HIS ONLY SON, OUR LORD

I BELIEVE IN JESUS CHRIST

To say "I believe in Jesus Christ" is a confession of colossal proportions. Many people hear the words "Jesus Christ" only as profanity. What a tragedy this is, because each of these words is bursting with meaning. Let us take them separately.

Jesus' name was given to him not by his mother Mary but by the angel who announced to her that she was going to have a son. He said to her, "...and you shall call his name Jesus" (Luke 1:31). The name "Jesus" is the Greek translation of the Hebrew name Yeshua, or Joshua. The name means "The Lord saves" or "The Lord is salvation." Immediately it raises this question: Saved from what? What does Jesus save us from?

An angel also appeared to Mary's husband-to-be, Joseph, in a dream. The angel told Joseph that Mary, his wife-to-be, had conceived by the Holy Spirit (more on that later). As the angel told Mary, so he told Joseph that he was to give the child the name Jesus. The angel went on to give the reason for this name: "for he will save his people from their sins" (Matthew 1:21b). The name "Jesus" means the Lord saves, and what he saves from is sin.

Now we have to ask more questions. What is sin? And how does Jesus save us from our sins? To answer these questions, we have to have a look back in history. Before we do that, however, we need to consider this other name, "Christ." Actually, it is not a name at all. It is Jesus' title. The word "Christ" is a title. It means "the anointed one." It is Greek for the Hebrew word "Messiah." Jesus Christ means Jesus the Messiah, or Jesus the Anointed One. Considering Jesus as Messiah takes us back to early human history. Keep in mind the larger question before us: What does it mean to be saved from sin?

How Sin Entered the World

God created our first parents, Adam and Eve, and placed them in the garden of Eden. God commanded them to work the garden. In so doing they would discover what God had made, and this would tell them more about God, which would please him very much. They were to have children and raise a family. Everything they did was dedicated to God. All that they learned told them more about the character of God. Adam and Eve enjoyed direct fellowship with God.

In the garden, God had given Adam a command: "And the LORD God commanded the man, saying, 'You may surely eat of every tree of the garden, but of the tree of the knowledge of good and evil you shall not eat, for in the day that you eat of it you shall surely die'" (Genesis 2:16-17). It was a test to see if Adam and Eve would obey him. It was a very clear command. If you do *x*, then *y* will happen. If you disobey, you will die. If we cannot understand this statement, we cannot understand anything. Then one day something terrible happened.

A creature called a serpent came into the garden. We don't know what this creature looked like originally. Most likely it was quite beautiful. Satan had entered this animal and he spoke to Eve through it. You might wonder why Eve wasn't afraid of this creature or startled that it could speak to her. What was there to be afraid of? There was no evil in the world that she knew. She was not aware of everything God had made and so this first encounter with a creature that could talk might certainly have been a curiosity but it did not present to her a sense of imminent danger. Whatever her initial feelings, the story in Genesis 3 does not show her being frightened.

The serpent approaches her and asks her a question: "Did God actually say, 'You shall not eat of any tree in the garden?'"

The woman, still appearing not to be frightened in any way, responds, "We may eat of the fruit of the trees in the garden, but God said, 'You shall not eat of the fruit of the tree that is in the midst of the garden, neither shall you touch it, lest you die.'" (Genesis 3:1–3). It seems to be a good answer, but Satan does not give up. He moves from planting seeds of doubt in her mind to telling an outright lie. "But the serpent said to the woman, 'You will not surely die. For God knows that when you eat of it your eyes will be opened, and you will be like God, knowing good and evil'" (Genesis 3:4–5). Now Eve has a problem. Whom is she going to believe? God said that when you eat of the tree you will die. Satan says you won't die.

Instead of depending on God, Eve decides to act on her own, to independently judge for herself between God and Satan. "So when the woman saw that the tree was good for food, and that it was a delight to the eyes, and that the tree was to be desired to make one wise, she took of its fruit and ate, and she also gave some to her husband who was with her, and he ate" (Genesis 3:6). Immediately they feel shame and guilt for what they have done. Their shame initially comes in realizing they are naked. Before this point, their nakedness has not been an issue. Now they immediately attempt to cover their nakedness by sewing fig leaves together. What is worse, they try to hide from God when he comes into the garden at the cool of the day. Apparently God appeared to them toward the end of each day and conversed with them. This must have been a most wonderful experience—think of it, to be able to speak directly with the creator of the universe! This time, however, the situation is much different. God calls out to Adam, "Where are you?" (Genesis 3:9).

God confronts them in their disobedience. They make up excuses for their action. Adam says it was the woman's fault. Eve says that Satan deceived her. For their sin, the ground is cursed such that humankind will work in sweat and toil from now on. The woman will have pain in childbirth. The worst thing, however, is that they are cast out of the garden, away from the presence of God, no longer enjoying direct fellowship with him.

Before God sends them away, he does something interesting. He kills an animal and clothes Adam and Eve with the skin. He does not accept their own attempts to cover their nakedness, that is, their shame. This is the beginning of what would be called the sacrificial system. From this point on, God would be approached in worship by means of a blood sacrifice.

What a terrible moment in their lives, forever etched in their memory. They had to leave the garden, and as they looked back, no doubt with longing eyes, they saw that awesome sight, an angel with a flaming sword, reminding them that the days of intimate fellowship with God were gone.

God in his holiness cannot tolerate sin in his presence. There was another tree in the garden called the tree of life. Eating of this tree represented intimate fellowship with God. Adam and Eve, in their innocence, would have been able to eat of that tree but now in their sinful state they forfeited that privilege. If they would have eaten of the tree of life, in their sinful state, it would have been such an affront to the character of God, thereby treating him with contempt, that they would have been forever condemned without recourse to salvation and the hope of eternal life with Him.

The Savior To Come

All was not lost, however. Remember that God had made clothing for them of animal skins. He, not they, covered their nakedness. The covering had to be done his way, not theirs. Then, something even more dramatic happened. God promised to send a Deliverer, a Savior. In this promise, God did not give much detail, but it was filled with hope. He said to the serpent, whom he also cursed for his role in deceiving the woman, "I will put enmity between you and the woman, and between your offspring and her offspring; he shall bruise your head, and you shall bruise his heel" (Genesis 3:15). Someday in the future, a child would be born whose heel the serpent, Satan, would bruise, but in the process, this child would crush the head of the serpent. Think about this. If you get injured in your heel, you can continue to function and the wound will eventually heal, but if your head is crushed, you are finished! This is what this child, who would be born sometime in the future, would do.

Meanwhile, the effects of sin on the human race continued to get worse.

In Genesis 4, we read about two sons, Cain and Abel, born to Adam and Eve. Cain, in a fit of jealousy, kills his brother. He does feel some remorse over this. We then read about a man named Lamech. Someone strikes him, obviously in some sort of dispute. Lamech retaliates by killing the man. He then brags about it. The effects of sin are being compounded. If someone hurts another, that person wants to exact an even greater injury, which may very well lead to murder. This condition of the heart is true of all of us in one way or another.

Since we are all of one blood, one humanity, we have inherited the sin nature of our first parents. Those effects are described here: "The LORD saw that the wickedness of man was great in the earth, and that every intention of the thoughts of his heart was only evil continually" (Genesis 6:5). We said earlier that sin is disobeying God. It is also a condition of our inner being—that which determines our outward actions. We commit sins because it is in our nature to do so. It is God who describes the effects of sin in us. Every thought, every intention, is bent toward disobeying God, all the time. We sin because we want to. We prefer it to obeying God. Yet, this is not the way God created us. All of creation was created good, including the first man and woman, who were made in the image of God.

It was a person that brought sin into the world. Sin is any lack of conformity to, or any transgression of, the law of God. To transgress means to cross a line from obedience to disobedience. We can sin by what we *haven't* done as well as by what we *have* done. Sin brought death into the world. "Sin came into the world through one man, and death through sin, and so death spread to all men because all sinned" (Romans 5:12). This death is more than just physical death. There is a resurrection of every person who has lived on the face of the earth and, after that, judgment. "And many of those who sleep in the dust of the earth shall awake, some to everlasting life, and some to shame and everlasting contempt" (Daniel 12:2). "It is appointed for man to die once, and after that comes judgment" (Hebrews 9:27). Jesus teaches us that there is a place of eternal punishment, a place called hell. It is a place "where their worm does not die and the fire is not quenched" (Mark 9:48). It is God's justice that says "the wages of sin is death" (Romans 6:23). Eternal punishment is the just penalty for sin. "The soul who sins shall die" (Ezekiel 18:20). What a dilemma we are in! We are inclined to sin, God holds us responsible for sinning, and the penalty for sin is death. It should be clear by now that we need a savior. We need someone who will save us from guilt incurred because of our sin and also who will save us from its grip, its destructive hold on our lives. We can't overcome sin by sheer will power. We need the power of the indwelling Holy Spirit who is promised to those who believe in Christ.

Our Need and God's Provision of a Savior

You may wonder why God did not send the Savior right away. While it is impossible to look into the mind of God in order to figure out why he does what he does, we do know that God was preparing humanity for the coming of the Savior. Over many centuries, it needed to be drummed into peoples' minds that there is only one God, maker of heaven and earth, who is holy, pure, and undefiled, who commands our submission, trust, and obedience. People needed to be reminded over and over that all other religions that worship other gods are false. "For all the gods of the peoples are worthless idols, but the LORD made the heavens" (Psalm 96:5).

In order to do this, God called a man out of the nations. From this man there came a family, then a nation which would eventually be ruled by a king. Some future day a descendant would sit on that throne as King of kings and Lord of lords. This is none other than Jesus Christ. It is important to fill in some of the details of the history that led up to the coming of the Savior.

In the previous chapter, we considered Abraham, who lived about 4,000 years ago. God promised that through one of his descendants, all the families of the earth would be blessed. Remember, there was already in human history the promise of a deliverer, a savior, made at the time when Adam sinned. Now God was going to begin to make good on that promise by calling Abraham (at that time his name was Abram) to leave his country to go to a land that he, God, would show him. From Abraham came the nation of Israel. They were the descendants of Jacob (whose other name was Israel), the grandson of Abraham.

Recall that we spoke of the descendants of Jacob being in bondage in Egypt. God remembered the promise he made to their forefathers, Abraham, Isaac, and Jacob. "And God heard their groaning, and God remembered his covenant with Abraham, with Isaac, and with Jacob" (Exodus 2:24). He raised up a leader, Moses, who would lead them out of Egypt. This was accomplished by God's "mighty hand and an outstretched arm" as he defeated the mighty army of Pharaoh when the Israelites crossed the Red Sea. You can read all about this in the book of Exodus. It was through Moses that God gave the Israelites (and us) the law as summarized in the Ten Commandments. This nation would be the bearers and preservers of the law, that is, the Scriptures and the covenants. Moses also spoke of the ancient promise of a savior. The ancient promise had not been forgotten by God: "The LORD your God will raise up for you a prophet like me from among you, from your brothers—it is to him you shall listen" (Deuteronomy 18:15).

From this nation would come the Savior who is Jesus Christ, born of the tribe of Judah. Israel went from being ruled by judges to being ruled by a king. The most famous kings were David and his son Solomon. David ruled around a thousand years before Christ. He wanted to build a temple, a permanent place in which to worship God. Up to this point, the place of worship was in a tent called the Tabernacle. God told David that he, David, would not build the temple but that his son, Solomon, would be the one to do this.

However, God made a most unusual and wonderful promise to David. He promised that his throne, his dynasty would never end:

> When your days are fulfilled and you lie down with your fathers, I will raise up your offspring after you, who shall come from your body, and I will establish his kingdom.

> He shall build a house for my name, and I will establish the throne of his kingdom forever.
> *(2 Samuel 7:12–13)*

For David, these words were just too good to be true. His kingdom would never end. It would last forever! The kingdoms of the world come and go, but this one would last forever. How? Looking at Israel's subsequent history, it is a wonder that this nation survived near extinction, let alone became a lasting kingdom.

In her later history, Israel forgot her God and acted like an unfaithful wife. God sent his servants the prophets to be the nation's conscience, but they would not listen to their call to return to the Lord. In anger toward the nation he loved, God uprooted her and sent her into exile, but left a stump, so to speak. In other words, the Jewish nation would not be completely annihilated. The temple was destroyed and all appeared to be lost. Yet God, in his providential guidance over the affairs of people and nations, returned her to the land in the time of the Persian Empire, in the fifth century BC. This brings us to the close of the Old Testament.

When we open the New Testament, some 400 years have transpired. We read not about Persians, but Romans. The Roman Empire ruled the Mediterranean world, including the province now known as Judea. But what happened to this kingdom that would never end? The one who claimed to be king of the Jews in Jerusalem was Herod, not a Jew at all, but an Idumean. (Idumeans were known in the Old Testament by the name "Edomites.") He was also a puppet of the Roman emperor Caesar Augustus. Most certainly he was not a descendant of David. What happened to David's throne?

Unknown to the world, in an obscure village in Nazareth, an angel named Gabriel appeared to a young virgin named Mary who was engaged to Joseph The angel told her that she was going to conceive and bear a son. Now consider the words of the angel Gabriel to her: "He will be great and will be called the Son of the Most High. And the Lord God will give to him the throne of his father David, and he will reign over the house of Jacob forever, and of his kingdom there will be no end" (Luke 1:32–33). Joseph, who became Mary's husband and Jesus' legal father, was a descendant of David. God did keep his promise to Adam, to Abraham, through Moses, to David, to the entire human race. Jesus Christ, the Messiah, the King of kings, would be born of the virgin Mary.

When the baby Jesus was presented in the Temple in Jerusalem, a godly man, Simeon, exclaimed,

> Lord, now you are letting your servant depart in peace, according to your word; for my eyes have seen your salvation that you have prepared in the presence of all peoples, a light for revelation to the Gentiles, and for glory to your people Israel.
> *(Luke 2:29–32)*

We saw earlier our need of a savior, one who would deliver us from the guilt and grip of sin. We also learned that from very early on a savior was promised. Look at Simeon's words: "[F]or my eyes have seen your salvation." Pause to reflect on this. Salvation is a person. It is none other than Jesus Christ, Jesus the Messiah, the one promised from ages past who would come to save people from sin and the condemnation that is the penalty for sin.

Let us gather our thoughts. The name "Jesus" means "the Lord saves." What he saves from is the penalty of sin, eternal death, and its corrupting effects on our inner being whereby we are always choosing to sin. The name "Christ" means Messiah, or "the anointed one." He is the one promised of God to come into the world to save sinners.

People have different opinions about who Jesus is. It was no less true in Jesus' day than it is today. He once put the question to his disciples:

> Now when Jesus came into the district of Caesarea Philippi, he asked his disciples, "Who do people say that the Son of Man is?" And they said, "Some say John the Baptist, others say Elijah, and others Jeremiah or one of the prophets." He said to them, "But who do you say that I am?" Simon Peter replied, *"You are the Christ, the Son of the living God."* And Jesus answered him, "Blessed are

you, Simon Bar-Jonah! For flesh and blood has not revealed this to you, but my Father who is in heaven."
(Matthew 16:13–17, emphasis added)

Now put the two together. To say "I believe in Jesus Christ" means that I believe that the person known to history as Jesus of Nazareth is the Messiah. It also means that I know I am a sinner and that sin has such a hold on me that, left to myself, I do what Adam and Eve did after they had sinned—run and hide—inventing all the clever ways I can think of to do this. It is to say that I need a savior and that Savior is Jesus *the* Christ. In other words, adding "Christ" on to "I believe in Jesus" means you are saying, "I believe that Jesus is the one of whom the Scriptures speak, whom God sent into the world to save sinners."

I Believe in Jesus Christ His only Son, our Lord

Now, that is a mouthful! Let us not pass over these words too quickly. What is being said in these words, "I believe in Jesus Christ *his only Son*"? We are saying that Jesus Christ is the eternal Son of God. The Apostle John informs us, "In the beginning was the Word, and the Word was with God, and the Word was God" (John 1:1). What is more, that Word which was in the beginning with God and was God "became flesh and dwelt among us." This can be none other than Jesus Christ. Think back to our earlier discussion about the beginning, the time just before creation. In Genesis 1:1 we are told, "In the beginning God. . ." Here in John 1:1, we are told that Jesus Christ was with God in the beginning. He has existed with the Father from all eternity. In other words, there was never a time when he did not exist.

In John 3:16, Jesus is referred to as "the only begotten son." The words "only begotten" speak not of some beginning point, but of his uniqueness. There is no one else like him. If there is no one else like him and he is eternal, then he is God. To say, "I believe in Jesus Christ his only Son," is to confess that you believe he *is* God. You are also confessing that he is fully God and fully man in one person. Let the Word of God speak to this:

> For in him the whole fullness of deity dwells bodily.
> *(Colossians 2:9)*

> For although there may be so-called gods in heaven or on earth—as indeed there are many "gods" and many "lords"—yet for us there is one God, the Father, from whom are all things and for whom we exist, and one Lord, Jesus Christ, through whom are all things and through whom we exist.
> *(1 Corinthians 8:5–6)*

One who is fully God and yet fully man is truly unique and, as we shall see, is fully qualified to be the Savior of the world. To say, "I believe in Jesus Christ his only Son," is to say, "I believe that Jesus Christ is the only one who can save me from the guilt and punishment of sin."

Since Jesus Christ is the only one who can save us, it follows that there is no salvation apart from him. As time went on in the ministry of Jesus, the more people heard his teachings, the more difficult it was to remain neutral toward him. He said some things that his hearers found hard to accept. For example, in one interchange he told his hearers, "Truly, truly, I say to you, unless you eat the flesh of the Son of Man and drink his blood, you have no life in you" (John 6:53). The thought of eating someone's flesh or drinking his blood is repugnant to anyone, but especially those to whom Jesus was speaking. He wasn't speaking literally; he was talking about following him and trusting him. His words, however, caused many to turn away. They left Jesus and no longer followed him. It must have been a very sad moment to watch people turn their backs on him and walk away.

Jesus then turned to his disciples and said, "Do you want to go away as well?" (John 6:67). No doubt it was a moment of decision; consider Peter's response: "Lord, to whom shall we go? You have the words of eternal life" (John 6:68). Peter is saying that there is no other way to be saved except through Jesus Christ. After the resurrection and ascension of Christ into heaven, Jesus' disciples went out to proclaim the good news of salvation. When they did this, it made their religious leaders very angry, and they were arrested and brought before them to give an account of their actions. Here is what Peter said to the religious council: "There is salvation in no one else, for there is no other name under heaven given among men by which we must be saved" (Acts 4:12). This language excludes every other way of salvation. To say "I believe in Jesus Christ his only Son" is to say that I believe he is the *only* way to be saved.

We add to the discussion here an additional truth of great significance. "I believe in Jesus Christ his only Son, *our Lord.*" When someone is a lord, he is master and owner. The title "Lord" in the Scriptures adds the notion of power, or, better said, *all* power, to that of being master and owner. "Lord," biblically speaking, refers to an all-powerful master and owner. In the previous chapter we combined two concepts, ownership and authority, into one word: sovereign. Here we might say that "Lord" refers to sovereign power, that is, ownership, authority, and all power. It now remains to understand "Jesus Christ his only Son, *our Lord.*"

In the Old Testament we find the name "Lord" many times. Of particular importance is the occasion God appears to Moses in the bush that is on fire but not consumed (Exodus 3). God is identified there as Yahweh, or Jehovah, which means, in Hebrew, "the one who is." Later in that same text, Moses asks for his name, to which God responds, "I am who I am" (Exodus 3:14). This is very close, if not identical, with the name Yahweh, which comes through in the English translation as "Lord." The name Yahweh, Lord, bespeaks a unique being that is more than the creator—one who defines all of reality. It is not that the Lord *exists*; but rather that the Lord *is*. As the Apostle Paul put to the philosophers in Athens, "for in him we live and move and have our being" (Acts 17:28). Thus, he has all sovereign authority, whether people recognize it or not. Shortly after this encounter with Moses, God set out to prove to Pharaoh very powerfully that he is indeed Lord.

Pharaoh was the king of the Egyptians. He had enslaved the people of Israel, who had been living in the land of Egypt for over 400 years. God had raised up a man named Moses to lead his people out of captivity, but Pharaoh was not about to let his slaves get away. God commanded Pharaoh, through Moses, to let his people go, but Pharaoh did not acknowledge the God of Israel. He had his own gods, and he even thought himself to be a god. Two of Egypt's other gods were the Nile River, which God turned into blood, and the sun, which God darkened. And worst of all, God struck Pharaoh's firstborn son dead. How would that be possible if Pharaoh himself was a god? He wasn't; he was a fake, a cheap imitation of the one true God.

The God who is revealed in the Scriptures is the only true God. This is what he says of himself, "For the LORD your God is God of gods and Lord of lords, the great, the mighty, and the awesome God" (Deuteronomy 10:17). Notice how this same description is applied to Jesus by the Apostle Paul: ". . . he [the Lord Jesus Christ] who is the blessed and only Sovereign, the King of kings and Lord of lords" (1 Timothy 6:15).

We have already seen how powerful the meaning of "Jesus Christ his only Son" is. It speaks of the historical person, Jesus of Nazareth, as being the unique Son of God Almighty, and, as such, eternally preexistent with the Father, and also as the promised Messiah, the only one who can save people from their sins. The title "Lord" provides an additional layer of understanding to this already awesome name, which, of course, is identical to who he is.

If God is the creator, and if he appeared to Moses in the burning bush identifying himself by the very special name "Yahweh," then God is Lord, that is, the owner and master of everything. The same can be said of his Son, Jesus Christ. He was there at creation; it was not his mere presence—he was actively involved in creation: "All things have been created by him and for him" (Colossians 1:16). Jesus Christ commanded the universe to come into existence. Therefore he owns the universe and everything in it, including you and me. He not only made everything, he holds it together: "And he is before all things, and in him all things hold together" (Colossians 1:17).

To say, "I believe in Jesus Christ his only Son, our Lord," is to confess with true believers in Christ throughout all ages that Jesus is Lord. The "our" in "our Lord" assumes that we are saying this with others, that is, we're saying this as a group. What group? We're talking about the church, people gathered around the truth that Jesus Christ is Lord. But to say that he is our Lord presupposes that you, as an individual, believe and confess that Jesus is *your* Lord.

The Apostle Paul tells us that "if you confess with your mouth that Jesus is Lord and believe in your heart that God raised him from the dead, you will be saved. For with the heart one believes and is justified, and with the mouth one confesses and is saved" (Romans 10:9–10). The heart and mouth represent your entire being, inside and out. These are figures of speech where the part stands for the whole, like "Give me a hand," or "Don't give me any of your lip," or "Do you hear me?" In the verse just quoted, the mouth stands for that which communicates with the outside world. Thus, it is more than just saying the words "Jesus is Lord." Our attitudes and our actions are also our words, because they also communicate something to people around us.

We confess that Jesus is Lord by what we say and what we do. Let's be reminded of what was just said—to confess that Jesus is *our* Lord assumes that he is *your* Lord. This is what is behind believing "in your heart that God raised him [Jesus] from the dead." The heart is the real you. It is the control room of your being. Everything you do springs from your heart. Have you ever heard the phrase, "His heart wasn't in it?" It simply means "He's just going through the motions." To believe something in your heart is to really, truly, and sincerely believe it. What is it that we're to believe in our hearts? That God raised Jesus from the dead.

What is the significance of believing in the resurrection of Jesus? Well, if you take away the resurrection, the truth of the gospel falls to the ground. We'll have more to say on this later. The resurrection is the part that represents the whole of God's story about his Son. To believe in the resurrection means that we believe everything the Bible has to say about Jesus. If Jesus did not rise from the dead, then he was just another human being, an idealist with good intentions who was killed by people who felt threatened by his agenda and his popularity. For example, one of his disciples, Thomas, would otherwise surely be wrong when he said of Jesus, after seeing the wounds of his crucifixion, "My Lord and my God" (John 20:28). Thomas, like all Jesus' followers at the time, was not looking for the resurrection of Jesus. However, when his followers encountered him risen from the dead, it transformed their lives.

There is a necessary connection between Jesus having risen from the dead and Jesus being Lord. You must believe it from the depths of your soul. It is an inner conviction. This is what enables you to say, "Jesus Christ is my Lord," so that you can publicly, together with his other followers, confess Jesus Christ as "*our* Lord." To the world we proclaim not only that Jesus Christ is our Lord but that he *is* Lord, by which is meant that he is Lord over all, whether people believe it or not.

For Further Consideration

1. Think of the life-altering choices you have made, choices that were made independently of what Jesus has said about how we should live.

2. What were the effects of those choices on you and on those close to you?

Prayer

I confess to you, Lord, that I have been living my life as if I'm the one in charge. Forgive me for ignoring your call to come to you to be saved from my sin and guilt. You promise a life that is abundant, that knows your love, and experiences the exhilarating joy of freedom from the destructive power of sin.

7

WHO WAS CONCEIVED BY THE HOLY SPIRIT, BORN OF THE VIRGIN MARY

Conceived by the Holy Spirit

Joseph, Jesus' earthly father, was engaged to Mary. Something dreadful happened—dreadful, at least, from the standpoint of Joseph and the rest of the community where they lived. Mary became pregnant before they were married, and Joseph was *not* the father. He would most certainly have to divorce her. In those days, promises to marry were taken so seriously that to break off an engagement was tantamount to getting a divorce. Since he was a kind man, he decided to do it privately so as not to publicly humiliate her.

One evening, Joseph had a dream. An angel of the Lord appeared to him telling him not to be afraid to take Mary as his wife, "for that which is conceived in her is from the Holy Spirit." The angel told Joseph to give the child the name "Jesus, for he will save his people from their sins."[2] This is the reason Jesus came to earth to dwell among us. As mentioned earlier in the last chapter, his very name means "the Lord is salvation." He came to save people from that which we are all guilty of. We are all sinners who have broken God's law. We need a Savior. So Joseph took Mary to be his wife after Jesus' conception. Moreover, we are told that Joseph "knew her not until she had given birth to a son. And he called his name Jesus."[3] They did not have conjugal relations

---

2 Matthew 1:20–21
3 Matthew 1:25

until after Jesus was born.

It is true that there are other miraculous conceptions mentioned in the Bible. Sarah, Abraham's wife, was beyond childbearing years and yet, by a miracle of God, she conceived and bore Isaac. The same was true of Elizabeth in the New Testament. She was the wife of Zechariah the priest, and she gave birth to John the Baptist. Though these conceptions were miraculous, in the final analysis, each was still a matter of the male sperm uniting with the female ovum through sexual intercourse to generate a new person, a human being inheriting the sin nature passed down to us by our first parents, Adam and Eve. The offspring, Isaac and John the Baptist respectively, great men as they were, like all of us were born sinners by nature and choice. With Jesus it was different.

That Jesus was conceived in Mary's womb by the Holy Spirit was something totally different, unique, without precedent, something that will never occur again. It was a matter of the eternal Son of God, who was without sin, leaving the glories of heaven and taking on a human nature. It was not a human becoming divine, such as the stories that can be found in pagan mythology. Rather, it was the divine nature taking on a human nature. The Apostle John writes, "And the Word [Jesus] became flesh and dwelt among us, and we have seen his glory, glory as of the only Son from the Father, full of grace and truth."[4] In this way, the child born to Mary was without sin. Jesus was indeed conceived in Mary's womb; he went through the period of gestation, followed by birth and growth to full maturity as a man. He also went through normal life experiences such as being hungry and thirsty, and becoming tired.

Jesus himself claimed to be without sin.[5] The Apostle Paul says that Jesus was without sin: "For our sake he made him to be sin who knew no sin, so that in him we might become the righteousness of God."[6] The Apostle Peter likened the death of Jesus on behalf of sinners to "that of a lamb without blemish or spot,"[7] meaning one without sin.

---

4   John 1:14; see John 1:1–14 and Philippians 2:5–8
5   John 8:46
6   2 Corinthians 5:21
7   1 Peter 1:19

The virgin birth of Jesus also tells us something very important about him. He was both human and divine. He was not half human and half divine, nor was he a blend of the two natures such that one could not tell one from the other. He was fully God and fully man, two natures in one person. How can this be? We can't adequately describe it in words. Ultimately it is a mystery. Yet the Scriptures make it clear that he is a divine person, truly a man and also fully God. This is important for the gospel. If God is going to save sinners, *he* is going to have to do it. We cannot save ourselves. Only God, the God-man Jesus Christ, is qualified to die for sinners. But the justice of God says that man has sinned and therefore man must pay the penalty of sin, which is death. Jesus suffered as a man, a sinless man, dying a real death on behalf of sinners. God's justice says that "the soul who sins shall die," and "the wages of sin is death."[8] By means of the finished work of Christ on the cross, salvation can be offered as a gift to anyone who will receive it by faith.[9]

Born of the Virgin Mary

The virgin birth of Jesus is very important for understanding why Jesus came into this world through the process of birth that you and I also went through. Remember, he is the eternal Son of God. In his divine nature, he has always existed. To put it another way, there never was a time when he was *not*.

What does this mystery of two natures, human and divine, in one person, have to do with you and me? God in his essential nature is unknowable. Why? Because we don't have any images in our minds which would enable us to describe him as he is in himself. We can imagine in our minds things large and small, hot or cold, bright or dull, but we have nothing in our minds that would enable us to figure out, on our own, who God is or what he is like as he really is in his essential nature.

That God the Son would come into this world as a baby having been born of a virgin means that we can really and truly know God. There is nothing like this in all the other religions of the

---

8   Ezekiel 18:20; Romans 6:23
9   John 1:11–12

world. Think of it. The eternal God, Jesus Christ, the Son of God, came into this world. He went through the stages of life that you and I have traversed. He lived among us. Like the rest of us he passed through childhood, adolescence, and on to fully mature manhood.

In his ministry, Jesus called twelve men to be his followers. They were special followers, more than classroom students insofar as they were learning as they lived and traveled with him. He taught people. He did miracles which demonstrated beyond any doubt that he was the Son of God. These twelve men, called disciples, gave us an eyewitness account of what Jesus said and did.

To believe in the virgin birth is also to accept the authority of Scripture. Matthew informs us that the virgin birth was in fulfillment of a prophecy made by Isaiah some seven hundred years before the birth of Christ.[10] "All this took place to fulfill what the Lord had spoken by the prophet: 'Behold, the virgin shall conceive and bear a son, and they shall call his name Immanuel' (which means, God with us)."[11] The question that you and I must answer when it comes to truth claims is this: What is your authority? In the physical world we need standards of weights and measures, without which we could not, for example, build a building or take someone's blood pressure. The same is true in the "metaphysical," the spiritual realm. There must be spiritual laws whereby we are able to relate to one another or take the measure of a person's character. What is true is ultimately based on authority.

Our authority for what is true, for what is right and wrong, must come from an unchangeable standard outside of ourselves; otherwise people would decide for themselves, based on their own preferences, what is right or wrong. Think about it. If no standard for morality exists, how would you know the difference between an act of charity and an act of selfishness? If people everywhere did what was right in their own eyes, it would lead to anarchy.

The eternal, unchangeable God has spoken. He speaks through his creation, in which we observe order, design, and laws of na-

---

10   Isaiah 7:14
11   Matthew 1:22–23

ture. He speaks through his Word written, the Bible, in which he gives us commandments by which we know what is good, right, and true. In the Bible, he speaks most loudly through his eternal Son, whom the Apostle John calls the Word, the Son of God. He, Jesus, the Son of God, is the central theme of all of Scripture.

It is by the Scriptures that we know who God is, who we are, the human condition, how we are to live, and what is our purpose and destiny in life. It is the Scriptures that declare to us that Jesus of Nazareth is the eternal Son of God born of the virgin Mary, thereby without sin, both fully God and fully man, qualifying him to be the Savior of the world.

For Further Consideration

1. Does any other religion in the world make the claim of God coming down to earth by being born of a virgin?

2. Given the reality that Jesus Christ is fully God and fully man in one person, is that a truth to be admired or one which demands a response?

3. It was at least three months into Mary's pregnancy (probably more) before she married Joseph. This would have created a social stigma for both Mary and Joseph insofar as it would have been impossible to explain that her conception was by the Holy Spirit. How would you respond in a situation conveying the appearance of wrong but where you are actually innocent?

Prayer

O Lord, I know that in this observable physical world there are things that even logic cannot explain. I conclude that there are many things in the spiritual, nonmaterial world of which I understand even less. I believe that you have made yourself known to us through the virgin birth of your Son, who became like us and lived among us. I want to know you, Lord. Help me! Give me understanding that I might fear your name.

8

SUFFERED UNDER PONTIUS PILATE

There was more to Jesus' suffering than the last few days of his arrest and subsequent trial under Pontius Pilate. He did, indeed, suffer under him, bearing the wretched cruelty of the Roman scourge, not to mention the agony of crucifixion—about which we will speak in the next chapter. Most of his earthly ministry was punctuated with suffering, mainly in the form of being maligned, misrepresented, and rejected. These were carried into his arrest and trial, where he experienced terrible physical suffering.

Some seven hundred years before Christ, the prophet Isaiah wrote about a suffering servant (see Isaiah 53). In the book of Acts, we read about Philip the deacon meeting up with an Ethiopian official, a worshipper of the God of Israel. He was reading from this very same passage in Isaiah. At that moment Philip, prompted by the Holy Spirit, was directed to join him in his chariot. Philip asked him, "Do you understand what you are reading?" The official sincerely wanted to know about whom the prophet was speaking. Philip proceeded to tell him that it was about Jesus, and he explained to him the good news about how he died for sinners and about how one becomes a child of God. The official received the message, and when they came to a place where there was water, he asked to be baptized. So Philip baptized him, and the official returned to his country rejoicing.

Here are some excerpts from Isaiah 53 that speak of Jesus the Suffering Servant:

> He was despised and rejected by men; a man of sorrows, and acquainted with grief.
> *(Isaiah 53:3)*

> Surely he has borne our griefs and carried our sorrows; yet we esteemed him stricken, smitten by God, and afflicted.
> *(Isaiah 53:4)*

> But he was wounded for our transgressions; he was crushed for our iniquities; upon him was the chastisement that brought us peace, and with his stripes we are healed.
> *(Isaiah 53:5)*

> All we like sheep have gone astray; we have turned—everyone—to his own way; and the LORD has laid on him the iniquity of us all.
> *(Isaiah 53:6)*

There is a connection, as we shall see, between Jesus' death on the cross and the forgiveness of sin. Very early in Jesus' public ministry, he encountered opposition. He had a way of getting to the heart of the matter. He pointed out the corruption of people's hearts. Many were satisfied with carrying out the rituals and ceremonies of their religion. Jesus didn't object to ceremony, but he objected to people worshipping God with their lips and not with their hearts. Let's face it: you and I have played the game of words without action. Jesus had a way of calling people out, and they didn't like it.

He would do miracles like healing the sick and casting out demons. On two different occasions he fed thousands of people, multiplying loaves and fishes from someone's lunch. That was enough for people to try to make him king. But Jesus saw through them. They wanted a leader who would deliver them from their cruel Roman occupiers. They were looking for political peace and material prosperity. He wanted them to repent of their sins and believe the good news that he could save them from the guilt and power of sin and eternal punishment.

As time went on, the Jewish leaders became increasingly hostile to him. They did not believe his message even though it was right out of the writings of Moses and the Prophets, which they said they believed. They were concerned that his popularity would stir up trouble and bring the Romans down on them as had happened many times in the past.

They had to get rid of him for the good of their country, so they felt. One of Jesus' disciples betrayed him to the Jewish leaders, who came one night with a group of soldiers to arrest him.

The next day they brought him before Pontius Pilate, the Roman governor. They accused Jesus of plotting a revolt against the Romans who were occupying their country. When Pilate questioned Jesus, he didn't agree that Jesus was guilty of trying to overthrow them. He saw him as just another one of the Jewish rabbis. He couldn't care less about what Jesus was teaching.

The Jewish leaders, who managed to stir up the people against Jesus, kept pressuring Pilate. He could not afford a negative report about him to get back to Rome, so he finally gave in to their demands to crucify him. Though it was clearly wrong for Jesus to be put to death, it was nevertheless decreed by God that he would die so that sinners might be forgiven. Why? If God wanted to save anybody, his justice would have to be satisfied. The just penalty for sin, as decreed by God, is death. Do you remember what he said to Adam in the garden of Eden? ". . . for in the day you eat of it [the Tree of Knowledge of Good and Evil], you shall surely die." (Genesis 2:16-17) He also says, "The soul who sins shall die" (Ezekiel 18:20). Man has sinned and man has to die. A finite person cannot die for the sins of others; only God can. Since Jesus is fully God and fully man in one person, he is qualified to die in the place of sinners, thereby satisfying divine justice so that he can offer the gift of forgiveness of sins and eternal life to all who will receive them.

Sin cuts through every one of us and has produced all kinds of suffering in this world. You have undoubtedly experienced suffering of one sort or another; or, people close to you, whom you love, have passed through this valley of tears, which has been a great source of sorrow for you. With great sorrow we see debilitating illness, terminal cancer, rejection of one sort or another, divorce, death, and tragedies that are only supposed to happen to other people. Remember, Jesus, the eternal Word made flesh who dwelt among us, knows suffering including the most dreaded human experience—death. "He took on flesh and blood that through death he might destroy the one who has the power of death, that is, the devil" (Hebrews 1:14).

Moreover, he became "a merciful and faithful high priest in the service of God, to make propitiation for the sins of the people. For because he himself has suffered when tempted, he is able to help those who are being tempted" (Hebrews 1:17-18). Think of it: through his suffering he made "propitiation," by which is meant that his death on the cross was a wrath-removing sacrifice. He is also a faithful high priest, that is, God the Son, Jesus, represents his people before God the Father presenting them holy and righteous on the basis of his death on the cross and enabling them to live the life to which he has called them. Jesus is truly "the founder and perfecter of our faith, who for the joy set before him endured the cross, despising the shame, and is seated at the right hand of the throne of God" (Hebrews 12:2).

For Further Consideration

1. Why do we react so strongly when our true motives are exposed?

2. How is it possible to read the Bible and yet miss its essential point?

3. Why did Jesus have to die?

Prayer

*O Lord, you are intimately acquainted with all my ways.
You know the thoughts and intentions of my heart.
I tremble at this request, but I ask you to expose the
condition of my heart as the beginning of my steps
toward knowing you.*

I Believe. . .

9

He Was Crucified, Died, And Was Buried

Jesus was crucified along with two criminals. Death by crucifixion is probably one of the cruelest forms of execution ever devised by man. The person to be executed was nailed to a cross by his hands and feet. This forced him to push his body up in order to breathe. Therefore, each effort to breathe was very painful. One of the English words for pain is the word "excruciating." It is a Latin-based word meaning "out of the cross." Sometimes the victim would hang for several days before dying by asphyxiation. In Jesus' case, he died in midafternoon on the same day, not because of the crucifixion itself, but because he laid down his own life, showing once again that he was both fully God and yet fully man in one person. His "Seven Last Words" (or sayings) on the cross point to his deity and humanity. We consider them here:

The Seven Last Words

It must be remembered that a man had sinned and, therefore, a man had to die, the just penalty for sin. No one can die in the place of another except Christ who was, and is, both God and man in one nature. As a perfect man, he had no sin. He did not die for his own sin. As the God man, he is able to die in the place of sinners, thereby satisfying divine justice.

"Father forgive them..."
(Luke 23:34)

And when they came to the place that is called The Skull, there they crucified him, and the criminals, one on his right and one on his left. And Jesus said, "Father, forgive them, for they know not what they do" (Luke 23:33-34).

Under the most unjust, not to mention, illegal, circumstances, Jesus, being nailed to the cross, forgives his executioners. It demonstrates his perfect humanity in his willingness and readiness to forgive.

"Today You Shall Be with Me in Paradise." (Luke 23:43)

"One of the criminals who was being crucified railed at him, saying, 'Are you not the Christ? Save yourself and us!' But the other rebuked him, saying, 'Do you not fear God, since you are under the same sentence of condemnation? And we indeed justly, for we are receiving the due reward of our deeds; but this man has done nothing wrong.' And he said, 'Jesus, remember me when you come into your kingdom.' And he said to him, 'Truly, I say to you, today you will be with me in Paradise'" (Luke 23:39-43).

Here we see the deity of Christ in his ability to not only forgive sin but to admit the repentant sinner into heaven. The second criminal recognized the justice of his punishment. That is true repentance. He also had the correct object of his faith, Jesus Christ, the only one who could impart eternal life.

"Woman, Behold Your Son." (John 19:26-27)

> . . . but standing by the cross of Jesus were his mother and his mother's sister, Mary the wife of Clopas, and Mary Magdalene. When Jesus saw his mother and the disciple whom he loved standing nearby, he said to his mother, "Woman, behold, your son!" Then he said to the disciple, "Behold, your mother!" And from that hour the disciple took her to his own home. (John 19:25-27)

How does one who is in such terrible, physical agony, think about any person besides himself? Yet here we see another example of the perfect humanity of Jesus insofar as he was thinking about basic family responsibilities. In this case, it was the care of his mother after he had gone.

"My God; My God. . . ?"
(Matthew 27:46, Mark 15:34)

Now from the sixth hour there was darkness over all the land until the ninth hour. And about the ninth hour Jesus cried out with a loud voice, saying, "Eli, Eli, lama sabachthani?" that is, My God, my God, why have you forsaken me? And some of the bystanders hearing it said, "This man is calling Elijah." And one of them at once ran and took a sponge, filled it with sour wine, and put it on a reed and gave it to him to drink.

This was Jesus' suffering in hell. We will speak more of this in Chapter 10. The turning away of the Father from the Son, the separation from the infinite love they enjoyed together from all eternity, was more agonizing than the physical suffering which was wracking his body.

"I Thirst."
(John 19:28)

After this, Jesus, knowing that all was now finished, said (to fulfill the Scripture), "I thirst." A jar full of sour wine stood there, so they put a sponge full of the sour wine on a hyssop branch and held it to his mouth.

Why bother to record a rather obvious detail amidst the larger picture of suffering and shame. It points yet again to his humanity. This might be an allusion to a psalm that is a lament of one who is alone and abandoned in his suffering, Psalm 69:21, "For my thirst they gave me sour wine to drink." The sour wine was for the psalmist, and Jesus, a fitting metaphor of drinking the bitter gall of abandonment, which, regarding Jesus, added to his suffering.

"It is Finished."
(John 19:30)

When Jesus had received the sour wine, he said, "It is finished," and he bowed his head and gave up his spirit.

On the face of it, it almost sounds like a cry of despair. To the contrary, it is a cry of victory. The Greek word is "tetelestai," which means, it is accomplished. The tense of the word conveys the idea that everything I have done regarding the work the Father sent me to do has been fully accomplished.

"Father, Into Your Hands . . ."
(Luke 23:46)

It was now about the sixth hour, and there was darkness over the whole land until the ninth hour, while the sun's light failed. And the curtain of the temple was torn in two. Then Jesus, calling out with a loud voice, said, "Father, into your hands I commit my spirit!" And having said this he breathed his last. (Luke 23:44-46)

Here in this last word, we see, once again, the deity and humanity of Jesus. He dies a real death as a man. Yet, as God, he lays down his own life; no one takes it from him. Earlier in his ministry he stated, "I lay down my life that I may take it up again. No one takes it from me, but I lay it down of my own accord. I have authority to lay it down, and I have authority to take it up again" (John 10:17b-18).

Crucifixion was normally reserved for the worst criminals. In his death, Jesus identified with the worst of sinners. "For our sake he made him to be sin who knew no sin, so that in him we might become the righteousness of God" (2 Corinthians 5:21). No one who wishes to come to him for salvation from the guilt and penalty of sin is beyond his reach as Savior. Salvation through Jesus Christ is freely offered to all—it is offered to you.

This was the time of the Passover, a very important Jewish holiday instituted by God through Moses, celebrating Israel's deliverance from bondage in Egypt. Every Jewish holiday pointed to some aspect of God's relationship with his people. During these special times, ritual purity was very important. The next day was a special Passover Sabbath and, therefore, according to ritual law, the bodies of those being crucified could not be left hanging during the Sabbath. It is a strange combination of events, Christ's crucifixion and the concern for ritual purity whose deeper meaning, throughout the history of God's chosen people, Israel, pointed to the very person they were crucifying, Jesus the Christ, meaning "Jesus the Messiah."

They could not wait for the normal progress of crucifixion. The soldiers came and broke the legs of the two criminals so that they could no longer push themselves up to be able to breathe. They died by asphyxiation. When they came to Jesus, he was no longer moving, that is, as indicated above, he was no longer breathing. They concluded that he was already dead, so there was no need to break his legs. This was to fulfill biblical prophecy that not a bone of his would be broken.[12] Just to make sure, one of the Roman soldiers pierced his side with a spear, out of which flowed blood and water. This is further proof that Jesus died a real death.

A further indication that Jesus died a real death is that his body was prepared for burial according to Jewish custom, and placed in a tomb carved out of rock. The opening was sealed with a large stone.

As noted previously, there is a sense in which Jesus did not really die by crucifixion. He laid down his own life. He is Lord, and no one can take his life from him. He laid it down freely, of his own accord. As was emphasized previously, he was (and is) fully God and fully man in one person. He alone has the power over life and death. His last words on the cross were, "It is finished," meaning "It is accomplished." What was accomplished? The satisfaction of justice. The just penalty for sin is death. Why? because God said so. "For the wages of sin is death, but the free gift of God is eternal life in Christ Jesus our Lord." (Romans 6:23) Jesus died in the place of sinners so that he could offer the forgiveness of sins and the gift of eternal life to those would receive him.

---

12   Psalm 34:20; John 19:36

FOR FURTHER CONSIDERATION

1. Under Roman law, death by crucifixion was reserved for the worst of criminals, the lowest of the low, the scum of the earth. Jesus not only bore the pain of the cross; he also bore its shame. No one in ancient times would dare to wear a cross as jewelry. How would you explain the difference between the ancient shame of the cross with its being a highly decorated artifact today?

2. Those who come to Jesus in repentance and faith could experience shame and humiliation or rejection of some sort. What would you say to a young man who believed the truth about Jesus but refused to be his follower because, in so doing, he would lose his inheritance?

PRAYER

O Lord Jesus, Son of God, Savior of the world, Lord over all, I confess that I deserve your just punishment because I am guilty for having broken your law. I am unable in and of myself to present to you any goodness from within that would obligate you to accept me as your child. Be merciful to me a sinner. I accept your work on the cross as sufficient payment for my sin and I confess that you are my Lord and my God.

10

HE DESCENDED INTO HELL

This phrase was added to the Creed at a later time[13] and inasmuch as it was written long after the Apostles had passed from this life, it has been subject to various interpretations. We mention two valid possibilities here.

This phrase most certainly does not mean that Jesus went to the place of the damned to suffer more punishment. We know from the book of Revelation that death and hades are cast into the lake of fire which is hell, an event to take place in the future.[14] Those, the living and the dead, who have not accepted Christ as Savior will one day, at the last judgment, be cast into hell. What has come down to us in the English language as "hell" was originally *hades*, the New Testament word for the place of the departed. The Old Testament word is *sheol*. We know from Jesus' parable of the rich man and Lazarus[15] that *hades*, before the resurrection of Christ, referred to a place for both the departed righteous and the unrighteous. They were separated by a huge chasm where there was suffering for those who, in this life, had not believed, and bliss for those who had. This latter part was called "Abrahams' Bosom."

The status now of those who die "in the Lord," that is, who die as believers, is that their spirits go immediately into the presence of the Lord, awaiting the resurrection of the body. Those who have died as unbelievers remain in hades also awaiting the resurrection of the body, at which time they will face the last judgment, to be cast into the lake of fire, that is,

---

13 Most likely around AD 700
14 Revelation 20:14
15 Luke 16:19-31

hell, the place of eternal torment.

Whereas it is true as previously stated, "he was buried," indicating that he died a real death, the phrase "he descended into hell" amplifies the reality of his death insofar as he experienced its humiliation, the separation of the soul from the body in the grave. This is not to be minimized because it reinforces the very important gospel truth that Jesus, in his humanity, died a real death in order to satisfy divine justice in the salvation of sinners.

Nevertheless there is a sense in which Christ suffered the torment of hell without going to the place of the damned, which, to repeat the point, will happen to unbelievers at the end of the age. Jesus Christ, the Son of God, in his humanity, was separated from the Father while on the cross. That separation was horrible for him. Think about it: he had enjoyed, from all eternity past, infinitely intimate love with the Father and now, on the cross, that loving relationship was wrenched from him. He experienced the wrath of the Father. He bore the just penalty for the sin of the world. The wages of sin is death.[16] That was the purpose for which he came.[17] At the beginning of Jesus' ministry, John the Baptist introduced him as the Lamb of God who takes away the sin of the world. How did he accomplish that?

In the garden of Eden, God told Adam that he could eat from fruit of all the trees in the garden except one, the Tree of Knowledge of Good and Evil. He warned Adam that "in the day you eat of it, you shall surely die." God means what he says. His words were not difficult to understand—even a child can understand them. The just penalty for sin is death.

God is a holy God. He is the creator and owner of the universe. He speaks and it is so. He spoke the universe into existence, which included the formation of our first parents, Adam and Eve, whom he fashioned in his image. He makes the rules because he is God. The penalty for sin is death because he said so. As we considered in the first chapter, he is Almighty God and doesn't answer to anyone else, because there is no other being like him, nor is there any being more powerful than he.

To our minds, such a penalty seems awfully harsh for stealing

---

16   Isaiah 53:4–6; Romans 6:23
17   Mark 10:45

some fruit off a tree and eating it. The problem is that in Adam's disobedience, the poison of sin entered the human race. A tiny bite from a rainforest mosquito can spread a poison into someone's body that ultimately can lead to physical death.

Adam did not drop dead the moment he ate the fruit. However, the process of death, that process which we call aging, where the body begins to shut down until it dies, began in his body and in his wife Eve's body.

What is worse, Adam and Eve were expelled from the garden. They could no longer be in the presence of God because God cannot live with sinners. Yet he did promise to send a savior who would, through his death on the cross, bring a portion of humanity back into fellowship with himself.[18]

---

18   Genesis 3:15

For Further Consideration

1. Why does the notion of hell fall so hard on our ears?

2. How can Christ's death on the cross displace our fear of death and the judgment to follow?

3. Who is the master of your destiny? How do you know that?

Prayer

O Lord, creator and sustainer of life, I confess that, left to myself, I would still be running from you, indifferent to the death wages of sin that otherwise loom over my life. Jesus, Son of God, grant to me the ability to hear your voice calling, and the eyes of faith to see my sin nailed to the cross.

11

THE THIRD DAY HE ROSE AGAIN FROM THE DEAD

The resurrection of Christ is the linchpin in the gospel account. A linchpin holds the parts of a machine or a system together. For example, linchpins can be used to hold a wheel to an axle. If the linchpin is removed, the wheel will come off, and the vehicle becomes inoperable even though the rest of its component parts are in order.

The resurrection of Christ is that part of the account that holds together and validates the entire gospel story, from God's initial promise to send a savior ("I will put enmity between you and the woman, and between your offspring and her offspring; he shall bruise your head, and you shall bruise his heel"[19]) to the coming of Jesus Christ into the world ("But as he considered these things, behold, an angel of the Lord appeared to him in a dream, saying, 'Joseph, son of David, do not fear to take Mary as your wife, for that which is conceived in her is from the Holy Spirit. She will bear a son, and you shall call his name Jesus, for he will save his people from their sins'"[20]). There is nothing like the resurrection of Jesus Christ in any other religion in the world. Whereas it is true that in some mythologies there are stories of the gods appearing on earth, or a person dying and becoming a god in the afterlife, there is nothing in the other religions about a person being born, a real human person who lived, died, and then came back to life, recognizable as the same person who had died previously.

19 Genesis 3:15
20 Matthew 1:20–21

If the resurrection did not happen as recorded in the Scriptures, then the entire story of redemption, which is the main theme of the Scriptures, falls apart. This was the Apostle Paul's argument. If Christ did not rise from the dead, then the message that is proclaimed about him is meaningless. What is more, our faith is meaningless. Simply put, if Christ did not rise from the dead, the Christian faith is false. But wait! That is not the worst of it.

There is still the problem of evil in the world. No matter what a person believes, he or she understands that evil exists. Apart from Christ and the Christian faith, what is the answer to the problem of evil? There are only a few possible answers:

1. *People are ignorant of what is good and right. Whereas this is partly true, the solution has been tried for centuries, down to the present day. "People simply need to be educated as to what is good and right," so it is often stated. However, more education has not resulted in lessening the problem.*

2. *People are stubborn. The solution to stubbornness, it is thought, is to persuade people as to what is good and right. Once they are so persuaded, they will do what is right. Some would go so far as to physically coerce a person into doing right. However, the problem with this solution is that as long as two people want the same parking space at the same time and it is the only space available, no amount of persuasion will convince either person to be nice and relinquish the space. The inevitable outcome is conflict, even violence.*

3. *The problem is a matter of the heart, because the heart is the control room of our being—that which makes us who we really are. It is what is on the inside that ultimately determines the choices that we make. It is in the nature of a pig to wallow in*

> the mud. It is in the nature of a cat to play with its captured bird or mouse before killing it. As the boxing trainer Cus D'Amato once said, "No matter what a person says, no matter the excuse or explanation, whatever a person does in the end is what he intended to do all along."[21] This is a good description of the condition of our hearts and the location of evil in us. It cuts through every one of us. It is a condition that is best described as being dead, that is, unresponsive to God's call, and with that, to how he wants us to live.

To summarize: The problem of evil is not a matter of ignorance (the supposed solution being information), nor is it even a matter of stubbornness, (the supposed solution being persuasion). Rather, the problem is found in the condition of our hearts—and our hearts control what we do outwardly. It is a condition that is dead, absolutely unresponsive to the things of God. Jesus describes it this way: "And he [Jesus] said, 'What comes out of a person is what defiles him. For from within, out of the heart of man, come evil thoughts, sexual immorality, theft, murder, adultery, coveting, wickedness, deceit, sensuality, envy, slander, pride, foolishness. All these evil things come from within, and they defile a person'" (Mark 7:20–23).

Please note that there is nothing here in your heart or my heart that would make us acceptable to God by simply being who we are from the time of our birth. But hold on—there is hope! Jesus told a religious man named Nicodemus, a Bible teacher, "You must be born again" (John 3:7b). That is one way of saying that we need a new heart, a transformation from the inside out. Only God can do that. This will address the basic problem of the human condition: guilt. In and of ourselves we are morally guilty for having rebelled against a holy and righteous God. It will also go a long way toward lessening the problem of evil in the world.

It is by means of the resurrection of Jesus Christ from the dead

---

21   https://www.goodreads.com/quotes/980926-no-matter-what-anyone-says-no-matter-the-excuse-or

that sin, death, and the devil were dealt a fatal blow.[22] It is because of the resurrection of Christ that you can be made a new creation in him, with a new set of values and a new desire to live for him instead of living for yourself, trying to create your own reality and choreographing your own happiness.

The resurrected Christ is calling you to turn away from ignoring God and living your own life your own way, to turn to him who offers you forgiveness of sin because Jesus Christ died in the place of sinners. His resurrection is proof that he can save you from the guilt of sin and also from its grip on your life. He offers you—as a gift—salvation from this guilt, and to bring you into his family by adoption as his child.

---

22   2 Corinthians 5:17

For Further Consideration

1. What does Jesus' resurrection from the dead say to us about how we are to receive what the rest of the Scriptures say about him?

2. Inasmuch as we all fear death, how can the resurrection of Jesus take away that fear?

3. Given the fact of Jesus' resurrection, is believing in him optional?

Prayer

O Lord, I admit that I suppress feelings that are indicators of something morally wrong in my life. I confess that those feelings are actually my guilt owing to my desire to live independently of you, making excuses for myself when I have broken your commandments. I accept your offer of salvation from my guilt and the forgiveness of my sins. I confess that Jesus is Lord, and I desire to learn how to submit my life in following him.

I Believe. . .

12

HE ASCENDED INTO HEAVEN. . .

HE ASCENDED INTO HEAVEN AND IS SEATED AT THE RIGHT HAND OF GOD THE FATHER ALMIGHTY

After Jesus rose from the dead, he appeared to his disciples and followers over a period of forty days. At the end of that time, he led his disciples to a place somewhere in the vicinity of the Mount of Olives, near the town of Bethany. There he blessed them and, in his glorified resurrected body, was lifted up into heaven. This event is known as the ascension.

It is an important event closely associated with the resurrection for several reasons: (1) He goes before his followers into heaven; (2) He is reigning now from heaven as king; (3) He is a perfect high priest who represents his people before the Father.

Jesus' death and resurrection secured the removal of guilt and the forgiveness of sins for those who come to him in repentance and faith, but in and of itself it did not secure their place in heaven. Before he went to the cross, Jesus told his disciples that he was going to go away to prepare a place for them where they would be with him forever. "In my Father's house are many rooms. If it were not so, would I have told you that I go to prepare a place for you? And if I go and prepare a place for you, I will come again and will take you to myself, that where I am you may be also."[23] This would include all those who would believe in him in the future. His followers will be with him in heaven forever.

But heaven is a pure and holy place where sinners cannot

---

23 John 14:2–3

dwell.[24] This situation originated in the garden of Eden, when our first parents sinned. Recall that they were cast out of the garden, away from the presence of God and away from eating of the tree of life which would have left them forever condemned. Remember that the penalty for sin is death, eternal death in hell. Jesus Christ paid that penalty in his death on the cross for those who would receive him. Not only does he forgive their sins; he adopts them as his children[25] and he credits his followers with his righteousness.[26]

A thousand years before the ascension, the psalmist asked this question: "Who shall ascend the hill of the LORD? And who shall stand in his holy place?" (Psalm 24:3). The hill of the LORD stands for the presence of God. If sinners cannot be in his presence—and we're all sinners—how can any one of us be in his presence? The psalmist proceeds to give the answer. Speaking prophetically, he presents the scene of Jesus' royal procession into heaven. He says, "Lift up your heads, O gates! And lift them up, O ancient doors, that the King of glory may come in. Who is this King of glory? The LORD of hosts, he is the King of glory!" (Psalm 24:9-10). The Lord of hosts is none other than Jesus Christ himself. Being fully God and fully man, he is the only one who, in and of himself, has clean hands and a pure heart. After all, he came from the presence of the Father and now he returns to his presence having accomplished the work of redemption that his Father gave him to do.

Jesus himself predicted his ascension when he told his disciples that he was going away to prepare a place for them. Since believers in Jesus are credited with his righteousness, as stated previously, they are able to enter the place he has prepared for them, that is, heaven.

Jesus' ascension means that he also is presently reigning as king. He sits at the right hand of God the Father Almighty. The right hand of the Father is a place of authority. The psalmist speaks of this in another place: "The LORD says to my Lord: 'Sit at my right hand, until I make your enemies your footstool'" (Psalm

---

24   Psalm 5:4–5; Revelation 21:27
25   Romans 8:15
26   Romans 4:20–24

110:1). Those who belong to Christ are not only his children, but are also his subjects. The Apostle Paul refers to this when he writes of Jesus sitting at the right hand of the Father, far above all rule and authority and power and dominion.[27] Christ's authority is absolute, and it stands above all powers and authorities in the seen and unseen world.

The Apostle Paul also declares that "if you confess with your mouth that Jesus is Lord and believe in your heart that God raised him from the dead, you will be saved" (Romans 10:9). The mouth is symbolic of what we are in public, that which communicates to the outside world by our words, attitudes, and actions. In other words, living under the authority of Christ the King will be reflected in our conduct. The way we act publicly is connected to the way we think internally, that is, to what we believe in our hearts. We have already noted previously that if the resurrection did not happen as recorded in the Scriptures, then the entire story of redemption, which is the main theme of the Scriptures, falls apart. The ascension reminds us of the resurrection and points to the kingly authority of Jesus. A follower of Christ lives under his rule and authority in every part of his or her life.

Having noted that the ascension means that Jesus has gone before his followers into heaven and that he presently reigns as king, it is equally important for him to be our high priest. A priest is one who represents the people to God. Since we cannot approach God on the basis of any goodness or propriety in and of ourselves, we need someone to represent us before his throne. Before the coming of Christ, in ancient Israel there were priests who offered sacrifices on behalf of the people. These sacrifices would take place if a person had sinned by breaking God's law. Sometimes the sacrifices would be for giving thanks or as an act of worship to God.

One very special sacrifice took place once a year, on a day called the Day of Atonement. The high priest, under very strictly controlled circumstances, would go into the holiest room in the tabernacle, called the Holy of Holies, and sprinkle the blood of a goat before the mercy seat. The mercy seat was a cover made of solid gold over a wooden box overlaid with gold, called the ark of

---

27 Ephesians 1:20–21

the covenant. The ark of the covenant symbolized the presence of God, and the sprinkling of the blood of the goat pointed forward to the blood of Jesus Christ, which he would offer in the presence of the Father in heaven. Whereas the animal sacrifices in the Old Testament were offered repeatedly, Jesus, our perfect high priest, offered his blood once for all time. "For Christ has entered, not into holy places made with hands, which are copies of the true things, but into heaven itself, now to appear in the presence of God on our behalf. Nor was it to offer himself repeatedly, as the high priest enters the holy places every year with blood not his own, for then he would have had to suffer repeatedly since the foundation of the world. But as it is, he has appeared once for all at the end of the ages to put away sin by the sacrifice of himself."[28]

Jesus' followers are comforted in the reality that he, their high priest, is interceding for them before the Father's throne, pleading the merits of his blood, by which is meant his life of perfect obedience to God's law for his people, and his death on the cross to satisfy the just requirement of God's law—because the penalty for sin is death.

Jesus, the eternal Son of God, ascended into heaven and sits at the right hand of God the Father, reigning as King of kings and Lord of lords. He is also continually interceding for his people as their perfect High Priest.

He is calling you to submit your life to him so that you will be a subject of his kingdom and so that you will know the forgiveness of your sin on the basis of his death and resurrection. He will then become your High Priest, representing you before the throne of God, whereby you will be enabled to live in him as his child and for him as his follower.

---

[28] Hebrews 9:24-26

For Further Consideration

1. *Jesus is calling you to come to him by acknowledging and repenting of your sin, by renouncing your desire to live independently of him, by bowing before him as your king, and by trusting in his promise that those who believe in him receive forgiveness of sin and the gift of eternal life.*

2. *Jesus in heaven is both King and High Priest. What do these titles speak to us about the accessibility of a holy God to sinners who, in and of themselves, cannot stand in his presence?*

Prayer

O Lord, maker of heaven and earth, you are God, and your Son, who is seated at your right hand, reigns as king forever. I acknowledge that I have been living my life in a manner that has disregarded you, your will, and your ways. I acknowledge this as sin, and I now come to you in submission to you as king. I trust in your death on the cross as sufficient payment for the guilt owing to my sin. I want to be your child.

I Believe. . .

13

FROM THERE HE WILL COME...

FROM THERE HE WILL COME TO JUDGE THE LIVING AND THE DEAD

When Jesus ascended into heaven, his disciples, who were standing there watching him go up into heaven, kept looking up as if he were about to return any minute. Two angels appeared to them and asked why they were standing there gazing into heaven. The angels assured them that Jesus would come back someday in the same way that he had gone up.[29] The Bible is clear that he will come again in his resurrected body. When he comes again, he will not slip into the world as a baby in a manger, but he will come in power, seated on a throne, and all the nations will be gathered to him.[30]

We are told in Scripture that it is appointed to man once to die, and after that comes judgment.[31] Many believe that when you're dead, you're dead. Yet, it is almost universally acknowledged that people fear death for the simple reason that, deep down, they know there is something beyond the grave.

Jesus spoke much about this. He said that he would come and will send out his angels who would gather his people and all nations before him. When that time comes, he will separate the believers from the unbelievers the way that a shepherd separates the sheep from the goats. True believers are people who have not only accepted what the Scriptures say about Jesus, but they have

---

29 Acts 1:10–11
30 Matthew 24:31
31 Hebrews 9:27

lived their lives in such a way that has shown they belong to him. In other words, the Word of God informed them about Jesus, and it formed their lifestyle according to his character.[32]

The last book in the Bible, Revelation, is written in even stronger language about Jesus coming again. It speaks of him coming with a sharp sickle in his hand to reap a harvest of those who belong to him and to gather the rest of humankind into the great winepress of the wrath of God.[33]

Those who belong to Jesus, who are living their lives in preparation for his coming, can look forward to a great wedding supper which will begin their lives with him forever in heaven, where God will wipe away all tears.[34] The rest, those who are not God's children by faith in Christ, will be thrown into the lake of fire, where they will be tormented day and night.[35]

---

32 Matthew 25:31–46
33 Revelation 14:14–20
34 Revelation 19:6–10
35 Revelation 20:7–15

For Further Consideration

1. If you are hearing the voice of Jesus calling you to come, then come! He promises that if you are thirsty, you may come and drink of the water of life, and you will never thirst again.

2. Coming to Jesus means going away from sin and the system of the world, which is a way of thinking that leads to a way of acting contrary to the will of God.

3. Have you ever reached an important goal in your life only to experience a great let-down afterward? After the great let-down now what do you do?

Prayer

O Lord, I hear your voice calling me to come. I am thirsty for you and I accept your invitation to come and to quench that thirst in my life, which is to know you in a way that will receive and experience your love.

I Believe. . .

14

I Believe in the Holy Spirit

The Holy Spirit is deity—fully God—along with the Father and the Son. No, we do not worship three gods; we worship one God who somehow subsists in three distinct persons, Father, Son, and Holy Spirit. One of the church fathers said that God is one in his "threeness" and three in his "oneness." We call this the mystery of the Trinity. It is a mystery because we cannot fully explain it, yet we can understand it to a certain extent. There is nothing unusual about knowing something truly without knowing it exhaustively. Scientists readily admit that there are many things in the physical universe about which we can know but which ultimately remain a mystery. If this is true in the physical realm, it is also true in the spiritual.

The Trinity is the unique God of Scripture. No other religion in the world has a god who is a Trinity the way he is described in Scripture. No other religion has a god whose members work in complete harmony with one another as do the Father, the Son, and the Holy Spirit.

We first read about the Holy Spirit at the very beginning of the Bible, in the second verse of Genesis 1: "The earth was without form and void, and darkness was over the face of the deep. And the Spirit of God was hovering over the face of the waters." The Spirit of God, hovering over this formless and dark space, was poised to inject life into creation, by which we mean a creation of order, beauty, and design governed by natural laws.

At this point we understand that we live in a moral universe, not an impersonal one made up only of energy and matter. You and I have concepts in our consciousness such as love, truth, justice, courage, etc. None of these nonphysical traits of human personality can be examined under a microscope, but we assume their reality by the way they are woven into every part of our everyday conversation and conveyed in our interpersonal relationships.

The Holy Spirit breathed life into creation in the sense that every particle in the universe exists to bring glory to God, that is, to show his power and majesty. This is especially true in the creation of our first parents, Adam and Eve, whom he created, male and female, in his image. God fashioned man out of the dust of the ground and breathed into him the breath of life by which he became a living soul. Whereas animals have lungs that function the way they do in humans, there is a qualitative difference between man and the animals. Animals do not create works of art, engage in science, write poems, invent machines, and organize groups of people around a common set of laws and beliefs.

The Holy Spirit generated life in the physical universe; he also gives life to those who are dead in trespasses and sin. When our first parents sinned, they were ejected from the garden of Eden—expelled from the very presence of God. We learn very early on the effects of sin. Every thought and intent of a person's heart is only evil all the time.[36] As we inherit the physical traits of our biological parents, so we inherit their sin nature as well. This means that when confronted with the truth about God, we suppress it. Moreover, left to ourselves, we don't like the law of God and we refuse to submit to him and his ways.[37] It is sad but true that the condition into which you and I were born was one of spiritual death, one where we were unable because we were unwilling and unwilling because we were unable to submit to God.[38]

Just as the Holy Spirit was there at the dawn of creation, infusing life into it, so he is also active in the new creation whereby people are brought from spiritual death to life in Christ.[39] It is the Holy Spirit who gives life to the one who believes in Christ. To have the Holy Spirit is the mark of a true Christian.[40]

36 Genesis 6:5; 8:21
37 Romans 1:18; 8:7
38 Ephesians 2:1–3
39 Romans 8:9–11; 2 Corinthians 5:17; Titus 3:5–6
40 John 7:37–39

This is the greatest blessing you can have. *First*, to have the Holy Spirit is to be assured of God's love.[41] What could be greater than to know and experience the love of the infinite, eternal God, creator of the universe? *Second*, the Holy Spirit is the seal of the believer's relationship with God through his Son.[42] A seal is something that guarantees authenticity. The Holy Spirit assures the believer that he or she belongs to Jesus. The Holy Spirit guarantees the believer of eternal life with Jesus forever.[43] *Third*, the Holy Spirit empowers the believer to live a life that is worthy of a follower of Christ.[44] The Apostle Paul tells believers in the church at Ephesus not to get drunk with wine but to be filled with the Spirit.[45] The Spirit-filled life is the Spirit-controlled life; it shows itself in the character qualities of Christ being lived out in the believer's life. The Holy Spirit enables the Christian to live like a Christian! *Fourth*, the Holy Spirit is a teacher as he brings to mind the inerrant and infallible Word of God which binds the conscience and enables you to discern truth from error.

41 Romans 5:5
42 Ephesians 1:13–14
43 Romans 8:12–17
44 Galatians 5:22–25
45 Ephesians 5:18-21

For Further Consideration

1. What does the Trinity say about the God of Scripture compared with the god(s) in other world religions?

2. How does the Holy Spirit enable a finite person to relate to the infinite God?

Prayer

O Lord, it seems impossible to live a life of love and purity, and peace and joy, but I thank you that you sent your Holy Spirit to empower me to live that life. Come, Holy Spirit, that I may know the nearness and the love of Christ who presents me faultless before the Father.

15

I Believe in the Holy Catholic Church...

I Believe in the Holy Catholic Church, the Communion of Saints

When the Apostles' Creed was in the early stages of its formation, sometime in the second century, there were major centers of the church—North Africa, Palestine, Asia Minor, and Europe. The word "catholic" by itself does not specify the church at Rome. It simply means "universal." That is the sense in which we are taking it here: "I believe in the holy universal church." The term "holy" literally means "separate." A holy church is comprised of people separated from other people by virtue of the fact that they are separated unto—that is, they belong to—their Savior, Jesus Christ. A member of Christ's church says, "I belong, body and soul, to Jesus Christ who loves me and gave his life for me."

You may sometimes hear a cynical comment made about the church that its members are comprised of hypocrites. It is sad, but true, that for every member of the church, there is a difference between what we say we believe and what we actually practice in our lives. It is also a fact that whatever a person's religion or belief system, there is always a discrepancy between what ought to be and what actually is.

We may think of the church in two ways: the church universal and the church particular. The church universal refers to all those throughout the world who believe in Jesus. They live under the banner of "one Lord, one faith, one baptism" (Ephesians 4:5). When we speak about the church particular, we are speaking about the same followers of Jesus Christ who meet together in specific local congregations or parishes. It is difficult to think of the one without the other. To be in the church universal is to be in the church particular. To be in the church in a particular location is to be in the church universal.

The church universal has in common with all churches throughout the world Peter's answer to Jesus' question to his disciples, "Who do you say that I am?" Peter's answer is the foundation of the church everywhere in the world: "You are the Christ, the Son of the living God" (Matthew 16:16). Jesus Christ himself is the cornerstone of this foundation, according to the Apostle Peter.[46] Peter further describes the church as a spiritual building, comprised of believers in Jesus as living stones built on the foundation that is Jesus Christ, a living stone.[47]

When the New Testament speaks about the church, it is usually in the context of a local, particular congregation, but never far from the notion of the universal church, the believers in Christ throughout the world. In addition to the Apostle Peter's description of the church as a living house comprised of living stones built on Christ the foundation, there is the Apostle Paul's analogy likening the church to a human body comprised of different interconnected parts, each dependent on all the others, and all the others dependent on each individual part. The church is to function as a body of coordinated parts, each helping the others to grow to maturity measured by the imitation of Christ.[48] This can only happen in a local church where the members know one another.

Additionally, we may speak of the church as a gathering of people in the name of Jesus Christ for (1) the ministry of the Word of God, (2) the administration of the signs and seals of our faith, baptism and the Lord's Supper, (3) fellowship, and (4) discipline—that is, helping individual believers to become more like Jesus in character.

The ministry of the Word of God is the most important activity of the church. It is multifaceted. It involves teaching, the

---

46 1 Peter 2:6
47 1 Peter 2:5
48 Ephesians 4:12–13

I Believe in the Holy Catholic Church. . .

setting down of the truths about Jesus Christ, who is the theme of all the Scriptures. It is also preaching, which is close to teaching and may even overlap with it, but which carries more of an appeal to the hearers of the Word proclaimed, calling them to put it into practice. Ministry of the Word can be very personal, such as in counseling. Worship as a congregational activity must be centered in the Word. There is also the activity of bringing the Word of God into the world, telling people the good news of salvation through Jesus Christ and living in practical obedience to the Word before a watching world by acts of sacrificial love.

There are physical, visible signs and seals of our faith. A sign is a physical object that points to, or confirms, something. A seal guarantees authenticity. It is something like clinching the deal, the way a signature functions on a contract. Water baptism and the Lord's Supper, partaking of bread and drinking wine or grape juice, are signs and seals of the Christian's faith. As signs they point to one's identity in Christ, and as seals they confirm one's identity in Christ, both on the basis of Christ's work on the cross. They are important because they are commanded by Christ, but the visible signs must not be confused with the spiritual realities to which they point. In the marriage ceremony, there are signs and seals of the marriage commitment; typically there is the exchange of rings and the signing of a marriage license which becomes a legal document. These signs and seals are very important, but only insofar as the realities to which they point.

We are warned in Scripture that it is possible to participate in the external rites of the church—baptism and the Lord's Supper—without truly being born again by the Spirit of God.[49] When one is baptized or participates in the Lord's Supper, that person is making a public statement about his or her relationship with Christ. God always takes our words, our public statements about being his child, seriously, even if we do not. Baptism and the Lord's Supper carry the force of vows, and God expects his followers to live out their baptism, their identity in Christ, and the Lord's Supper, living in daily fellowship with him in a life of repentance, faith, and service.

Fellowship is another important aspect of the church. The

49 1 Corinthians 10:1–3

word "fellowship" often conveys the idea of a social gathering where people drink coffee, enjoy sweets, and exchange pleasantries. The biblical meaning of the word is, however, much deeper. In the early church there were those assigned to "serve tables." This is a figure of speech where the part stands for the whole. In other words, it carries with it the idea of caring and sharing, meeting needs, typically basic and practical needs, whatever they might be. This might entail caring for the sick, helping with emergency financial needs such as purchasing groceries or helping to pay medical bills, or caring for children while Mom is in the hospital. Members of the church have a responsibility to care for one another in acts of sacrificial love.[50] These acts are to extend beyond the church and should affect the world at large.

Thus far, we have dealt with the church's ministry of the Word of God, the administration of the signs and seals of baptism and the Lord's supper, and fellowship. Finally, it is the church's responsibility to exercise discipline. In any relationship, be it among family members, coworkers on the job, or neighbors in your community, there is the need to act properly and responsibly toward one another, depending on the relationship.

The discipline that the church exercises is both positive and negative. Positive discipline takes on the form of encouragement and motivation. When we come together, we are to spur one another on to love and good works.[51] This is somewhat similar to going to an athletic competition where we cheer for our favorite team or competitor. Positive discipline is one of the ways we show love to one another.

Though it seems contrary to our way, negative discipline is yet another way to show love to one another. Negative discipline involves correcting a church member, one who confesses Christ to be Lord of his life but who is bringing public shame on the name of Jesus Christ by the way he is talking or acting. This does not mean that the church takes action on a member for every minor infraction. Whereas it is the church's responsibility to help its members learn how to deal with various kinds of sin in their lives, what is in view here is the kind of sin that undermines an

---

50 Luke 10:27-37; 1 John 4:7-8
51 Hebrews 10:24–25

appropriate example of the gospel. It is a sin or a pattern of sin that negatively affects the offender's testimony before a watching world, and seriously affects the spiritual wellbeing of the offending believer.

The Word of God provides a firm but loving way to deal with the offender. If one sees a fellow church member sinning in a manner that brings public reproach on the name of Christ, that person is to go to the offender privately, humbly, prayerfully, lovingly, and with the motivation to see that person restored and healed.[52] There is a procedure to follow that is given by our Lord himself. The person who brings the accusation must seek to deal with the matter privately, without involving anyone else who is not part of the problem or the solution. If one is unable to address the matter privately, then it becomes public. If the offender is still not repentant, he or she is to be put out of the church.[53] This is not to punish the person, but to make the offender feel the effects of being apart from Christ and his people so that they would want to return and give evidence of true repentance. The motivation for this kind of discipline is always to achieve healing and restoration to fellowship in the church and, most importantly, to fellowship with Christ.

With this fourfold description of the church: ministry of the Word, the signs and seals, fellowship, and discipline, we can begin to understand the idea of "the communion of saints." We need to explain our terms here. The word "communion" literally means "one with." Being one with, or in communion with, another person or a group of people is seen in many aspects in life. Workers constructing a building, musicians in an orchestra, players on a sports team, all have to be one with each other in order to complete the task, play the music, or win the game. That oneness involves different tasks functioning together to achieve a common purpose. The human body is made up of many parts, most of which are very different from one another, yet they function together to produce one coordinated body. It's not surprising, then, to find the Apostle Paul comparing the local church to the human body.[54]

---

52 Galatians 6:1
53 Matthew 18:15–20
54 Romans 12; Ephesians 4

Then there is the communion of saints. What is a saint? The word in this context is not referring to a special class of Christian who is more holy than the average believer. In its original formation, it was another word for a follower of Christ, a member of the church. In the Apostle Paul's letters to the churches, he uses the word "saints" in addressing the believers. The root meaning of the word is "holy," which means to be set apart. It is a good description of the followers of Christ. A Christian is one who is set apart to and for Christ. Simply put, a saint, according to Paul's usage, is one who belongs to Jesus Christ.

We have already alluded to the communion of saints in the discussion above about fellowship, which refers to caring and sharing, together with discipline, which involves encouraging or warning. In both situations there is a communion, a *one-with-ness* of believers in the church.

"The communion of saints" refers to believers in Christ who are committed to one another by virtue of their commitment to Christ. There is a vertical as well as horizontal aspect to this communion. This is more than people having a common interest, like members of a stamp collecting club or model train club. At a ball game, you may join everyone cheering for the home team, but beyond that there is no commitment to those around you.

This communion, or oneness, was an important theme in our Lord's prayer before he went to the cross. He prayed that they, his followers, would be one as the Father and Son are one.[55] This is beautifully illustrated when believers in the church partake of the Lord's Supper, each partaking from one loaf and drinking from one cup, declaring our union with Christ by virtue of his suffering and death on behalf of his people, and, thereby, our union with our fellow believers.[56]

---

55 John 17:11
56 1 Corinthians 10:16–17

For Further Consideration

1. What is the difference between the church as a community of believers in Christ and, say, a tennis club or a political club?

2. Fellowship, or communion, with Christ necessarily places a follower of Christ in the worshipping community of believers called the church. How does this work against the hyper-individualism of the present age—to the advantage of the believer?

Prayer

Lord, help me to engage with your people as a fellow traveler on this journey to the "Celestial City," as we worship you, serve you, and bear one another's burdens out of love for you.

I Believe. . .

16

I Believe in the Forgiveness of Sins

Virtually everyone agrees that sin is bad. But why? Recall the chapter on the first statement of the confession, "I believe in God, the Father Almighty." There we saw that God is holy. The holiness of God speaks of his uniqueness. There is no other being like him. We also noted that holiness, with respect to God, speaks of his purity; there is no defect, no evil in him whatsoever. It also assumes his authority over our lives. He is the ultimate authority in the cosmos.

Moreover, he is the creator, and he made human beings, you and me, male and female in his image. That establishes his ownership and authority over our lives. To our first parents, Adam and Eve, in their state of innocence, God gave a command: "And the Lord God commanded the man, saying, 'You may surely eat of every tree of the garden, but of the tree of the knowledge of good and evil you shall not eat, for in the day that you eat of it you shall surely die'" (Genesis 2:16–17).

When Satan came into the garden to tempt them, Adam and Eve decided that they would be their own authority, deciding between God and Satan as to who was right. This was the beginning of their sin, which led to their act of disobedience in eating the forbidden fruit.

Being descended from our first parents, we have inherited their guilt together with a preference for sinning. We are sinners by nature and choice, by which is meant we commit sins because it is in our nature to do so.[57]

The penalty for sin is death. Suffering and death in this world are the results of sin. Physical death is not the end; there is judg-

---

57 Genesis 6:5; Mark 7:21–23; Romans 3:23

ment to follow.[58] There is a second death for those who die in their sin.[59] It is called hell, a place of eternal conscious suffering. We learn about this mainly from the teachings of Jesus himself.[60]

The Scriptures are quite clear. This matter comes from the mouth of God himself—the penalty for sin is death.[61]

But wait! There is forgiveness for sin. That is what the gospel, which means good news, is about. The Apostle Paul expresses it quite simply in his letter to the Corinthians: "For I delivered [the gospel] to you as of first importance what I also received: that *Christ died for our sins* in accordance with the Scriptures" (1 Corinthians 15:3, emphasis added). How does Christ dying for sinners bring about forgiveness? Death is the penalty for sin. Jesus' death and resurrection paid the penalty for sin. The justice of a holy God has been satisfied. "For our sake he made him to be sin who knew no sin, so that in him we might become the righteousness of God" (2 Corinthians 5:21).

Jesus Christ—the divine person, fully God and fully man—in his humanity, by means of his death and resurrection from the dead, paid the penalty for sin. The psalmist says it beautifully and succinctly: "Blessed is the one whose transgression is forgiven, whose sin is covered" (Psalm 32:1). How blessed indeed!

Those who will receive him as Lord and Savior are released from the guilt of their sin. They are now free to follow him in order to be delivered from the grip of sin and to serve him out of love for him.[62] In one sense, it can be said that forgiveness is not enough. If, after due process in a court of law, one is declared not guilty, that verdict in and of itself it says nothing about that person's character and subsequent lifestyle. Not so with the gospel. The believer in Christ is saved from sin unto good works.[63] The purpose of God's forgiveness is that the one forgiven can live a life of holiness, purity, and self-sacrificing love.[64]

58　Daniel 12:2; Hebrews 9:27; Revelation 20:12
59　Revelation 20:11–15
60　Matthew 8:12; 13:47–50; 22:11–14
61　Ezekiel 18:20; Romans 6:23
62　Ephesians 5:1
63　Ephesians 2:8–10
64　1 Peter 2:24

For Further Consideration

1. You might be tempted to believe, "I am such a horrible sinner that I am beyond being forgiven by God." Is there any sin so terrible that it is beyond the reach of the grace of God?

2. Evaluate the oft-repeated statement, "I know God forgives me, but I haven't been able to forgive myself." What does such a statement say about the sufficiency of God's forgiveness?

Prayer

Lord, I admit that I have engaged in the pleasures of sin, thinking of myself first and others last, least of all you. My futile attempts to deaden the pain of my guilt by suppressing the truth that comes from you have not produced the desired result. Much less have they healed the emptiness in my own life and the injury I have caused in broken relationships. I now confess my need of you, and I accept your offer of forgiveness because I now see, through the eyes of faith, that you have borne my sin in your body on the cross.

I Believe...

17

I Believe in the Resurrection...

I Believe in the Resurrection of the Body, and the Life Everlasting. Amen.

The popular attitude toward death these days is either dismissive ("When you're dead, you're dead.") or like whistling in the dark ("He/she is in a better place."). People fear death because deep down they fear that there is something ominous beyond the grave. There is indeed. The reality of the resurrection runs deep in human history. Job, writing around 2,000 years before the times of Christ, said, "For I know that my Redeemer lives, and at the last he will stand upon the earth. And after my skin has been thus destroyed, yet in my flesh I shall see God" (Job 19:25-26).

The prophet Daniel, writing about 550 years before Christ's birth, states it clearly: "And many of those who sleep in the dust of the earth shall awake, some to everlasting life, and some to shame and everlasting contempt" (Daniel 12:2). Again, in the New Testament, "Whoever believes in the Son has eternal life; whoever does not obey the Son shall not see life, but the wrath of God remains on him" (John 3:36); and "It is appointed for man to die once, and after that comes judgment" (Hebrews 9:27).

We learned in previous chapters that Jesus rose from the dead in a glorified resurrected body and that he ascended into heaven as his disciples looked on.[65] Before he went to the cross, he told his hearers that he was going to come again.[66] When he comes again, he will come in glory and power like a mighty army, with

---

65 Matthew 28; Mark 16:1–8; Luke 24; John 20–21; Acts 1:1–11
66 Matthew 25:31–46; John 14:1–6

his angels. He will sit on a throne and all the peoples will be gathered to him, at which time he will separate the "sheep" from the "goats," by which is meant the true followers of Christ will be separated from those who are not his followers. In other words, there is a resurrection of the body for all people, the righteous and the unrighteous. Those who are not followers of Christ will be thrown into the lake of fire, hell. It is a place of everlasting torment.[67]

For the follower of Christ, there is a resurrection of an imperishable body, that is, a body that will never decay or be racked with pain and disease. Here is how the Apostle Paul says it: "Behold! I tell you a mystery. We shall not all sleep, but we shall all be changed, in a moment, in the twinkling of an eye, at the last trumpet. For the trumpet will sound, and the dead will be raised imperishable, and we shall be changed" (1 Corinthians 15:51–52). It is everlasting life, a life of eternal happiness with the Lord Jesus Christ.

> And I heard a loud voice from the throne saying, "Behold, the dwelling place of God is with man. He will dwell with them, and they will be his people, and God himself will be with them as their God. He will wipe away every tear from their eyes, and death shall be no more, neither shall there be mourning, nor crying, nor pain anymore, for the former things have passed away."
> *(Revelation 21:3–4)*

---

[67] Mark 9:42–48; Luke 16:19–26; Revelation 20:14–15

For Further Consideration

1. *The question you have to face is whether you will die in a state of grace, where your sins are forgiven, or in the state in which you (as we all) were born, where the wrath of God remains on those who have not accepted Christ as Savior and Lord.*[68]

2. *How will you know the answer to this question for you personally?*

Prayer

Lord Jesus Christ, I now see that my eternal destiny is in your hands, because you will come again to reconcile all of humanity and creation to conform to your holy will. I want to be numbered among those who will be raised to an imperishable life that is eternal in your glorious presence.

---

68 John 3:36

I Believe...

18

Conclusion

I have set before you the basics of the Christian faith, what most Christians of whatever conviction, high church or low church, have confessed believed for nearly two thousand years. To be a true follower of Christ, however, is not simply a belief in a set of propositions about Christ and the Christian faith. It is a commitment of the heart that leads to a change of life that is consistent with being a follower of Jesus. The heart is the real you, the control room of your being. We do nothing but what our hearts tell us to do. In the gospel, God promises to change our hearts, thereby enabling us to trust and obey him.

Jesus says, "Come to me, all who labor and are heavy laden, and I will give you rest. Take my yoke upon you, and learn from me, for I am gentle and lowly in heart, and you will find rest for your souls. For my yoke is easy, and my burden is light" (Matthew 11:28-30). That restlessness you are now feeling is the indication of a life that is separated from God because of your sin. Jesus not only offers forgiveness, but also adoption as his child, enabling you to follow him and walk with him through the storms of life and to live in his love for you and seek to love him in return.

I hope you are not one of those who, deep down, feel that they would be doing God a favor by turning to him and following him. To the contrary, he would be doing you a favor. This favor is called grace. Yes, there is that wonderful promise in John 3:16, "For God so loved the world that he gave his only Son, that whoever believes in him should not perish but have eternal life." Again, to believe in him is a commitment that involves our entire being, the heart as well as the head. Yet in that same chapter in John's Gospel, John 3:36, we have a warning. "Whoever believes in the

Son has eternal life, whoever does not obey the Son shall not see life, but the wrath of God remains on him." No. You're not doing God a favor. He's doing you a favor. He promises forgiveness of sin, adoption as his child, a life of joy, purpose, and eternal life with him forever.

Come to him in repentance. This means having a change of mind that leads to a change in living. Come to him in repentance and faith. Faith is believing the promises of God and living by them. "The just shall live by faith" (Romans 1:17b, KJV). It is accepting as true everything in the Word of God, especially that which reveals God to us and how he has reconciled sinful humanity to himself. It is believing that God has forgiven my sins because his justice has been satisfied on the basis of the life, death, and resurrection of Jesus. It is believing that Christ dwells in my heart because of the indwelling presence of the Holy Spirit who unites me to the Christ in heaven, who presents me as holy before the Father.

He is calling you to come to him now.

About the Author

Robert Hall was co-pastor of The Bronx Household of Faith, an urban church in New York City, until his retirement in 2018. He was born in Minneapolis, Minnesota.

He is a graduate of the University of Minnesota and earned a Master of Divinity degree from Covenant Theological Seminary in St. Louis and a Master of Theology degree from Westminster Theological Seminary in Philadelphia. He is an ordained minister in the Conservative Congregational Christian Conference (CCCC) and formerly served as its area representative for the Greater New York/New Jersey area.

www.ingramcontent.com/pod-product-compliance
Lightning Source LLC
Chambersburg PA
CBHW071213070526
44584CB00019B/3020